CANCER

My Teacher, My Healer

MANUELA SHERMAN

M S P

MSP

Manuela Sherman Publications
manuelasherman@gmail.com

Amazon.com / CreateSpace.com

Cancer, My Teacher, My Healer / Manuela Sherman
Memoir/Literature. Health and Medicine/Cancer

ISBN-13: 978-1500373528
ISBN-10: 1500373524
Cover design: Kerry Ellis, www.kerryellis.com
Sunrise photo by Yiota Kutulas

To Victor
whose life just started

and inspired mine.

INTRODUCTION

Gilbert Renaud, Ph.D.

I remember saying to Manuela Sherman, "We need you to write a book. We need you to tell us how you have been able to overcome the obstacles you have faced in your life and how you overcame cancer." She was surprised. She said she could never imagine herself actually writing a book. At that moment, setting such a lofty goal seemed preposterous and overwhelming to her. Things have certainly changed since the time I made that suggestion. Now I am honored to introduce the book Manuela has written: the story of a remarkable woman who took charge of her own healing.

Manuela Sherman, known as Manoli to her friends, has studied Recall Healing with me for several years. Recall Healing, the healing modality I integrated as a result of my own studies, is concerned with discovering and treating the cause of our illnesses. I believe that only when the cause is discovered and treated can true healing occur. Manoli studied Recall Healing 1, 2 and 3 with me in addition to a course on dreams and a course on releasing trauma. We also had six private sessions together. When Manoli asked me to read this book, her "healing journey with cancer," I accepted her request with enthusiasm. I received her manuscript, read it, and was absolutely riveted. As a therapist, I recognized the enormity of the actions she took to heal. I came to understand and deeply appreciate her long moments of solitude, her unwavering determination, her passion for new discoveries in life and for new subjects to study and explore. For example, Manoli describes a long period where she is alone in the process without much support, all the while witnessing other friends and patients dying. Despite these obstacles and more, however, she kept going. Where did she get her determination? You will see in her book how she develops a great fortitude and the ability to go on.

In her book, Manoli talks about her existence from before and at birth, and how the later events in her life shaped the woman she is today. The story she tells is intense—and she keeps it flowing with a great rhythm, simplicity and truth.

When I studied naturopathy years ago, I remember reading about a study done by Deepak Chopra. At the time, there were strong medical data and statistics describing the situations and choices of people who did not survive critical medical conditions. Chopra decided to study people who *had* survived these serious medical conditions to find out what they did differently from the non-survivors. He concluded that the survivors had two things in common:

> 1. They changed their perception of the conflicting situation they experienced at the moment they got sick;
> 2. They modified their behavior and adopted a new lifestyle.

These common themes stayed in my mind and became central to my work with my clients.

In Recall Healing we do not interfere with medical diagnoses or protocols; following selected procedures is a precious and primary action for the patient to take. Our job, however, is to discover and heal the emotional trauma behind illness, and, in that process, to alter the behavioral patterns that give rise to illness in the first place. We notice that when the underlying emotional trauma behind the medical condition is identified and resolved, the healing process can be set in motion—powerfully. Why? Simply because the common belief for most people is this: when we get sick, we feel "victimized." We believe we "caught it from someone"… "somewhere." In Recall Healing, we help clients transcend the sense of victimization by becoming aware of the emotional trauma underlying their condition—emotional trauma from their own lives. We help people remember personal experiences which were extremely stressful; we help people remember situations that remain unresolved. Although it is not an absolute fact, the illness that manifests is most often related to that trauma. Though we are aware that there are many ways to become ill and also many ways to heal, over the last thirty years in my practice, I have observed the presence of intense emotional trauma in over ninety percent of my clients.

Recall Healing integrates recommendations for healing from the great psychiatrist Carl G. Jung. These recommendations break down into three important steps:

1. The conflicting situation (trauma) behind the condition must be identified;
2. Appropriate action must be taken to resolve the trauma. This includes entering into an effective medical protocol, an effective diet, appropriate physical exercises and relevant therapies;
3. The afflicted person must persevere in the healing process. Keep going! Most people get sick after years of repeating the same life patterns. Most of us secretly wish to heal inside of one or two weeks without making the necessary changes to rectify the conditions that have contributed to our illness. This is why perseverance is so important. Serious illnesses do not heal overnight. True healing requires changing patterns; making conscious choices and pursuing new life designs over time.

In healing her cancer, Manuela Sherman identified the source of her illness, employed effective protocols to treat the causes, and persevered in developing and maintaining a new lifestyle. In this book she shares her process, a process which ultimately allowed her to become an "observer" of her own life. When you learn how to observe your own behavior, things start to "shift." Manoli observed her life and began to change her perspective. She emerged with a completely new sense of her own identity. As a result of this deep introspection, she healed herself from cancer.

I have learned some important things from this book. The most important thing I learned, as a professional healer, was to recognize how much support a client may need during the course of her or his illness. I have become a much more involved therapist. The path to healing can be depressing. At times people feel hopeless—but, as Manoli shows us, there is hope. The key is perseverance. In this book she shows us how one person did it.

Manoli, I honor you for what you have done and for what you have taught me. I am in deep appreciation.

Now, dear reader, I wish you healing, and, as part of that path, I am honored to invite you to enter into the wisdom of Manuela Sherman's Healing Journey.

TABLE OF CONTENTS

PROLOGUE
A Leap of Faith

Manuela Sherman

In Spain where I was born, they say "There are three things you must do before you die: Have a child, write a book and plant a tree." I heard this many times as I was growing up. I was adamant I was never going to do any of them. The truth is I hated this world so much I was firmly committed, first, to die young and, second, to leave no trace.

From the beginning, I knew this was not going to be an easy life. I had chosen illness, or illness had chosen me, to learn my life lessons. I was born with congenital heart anomalies. That would set my course in life.

Eventually I would grow spiritually. Eventually I would awaken. Eventually I would learn how to *live*, meaning I would begin to understand myself—from the point of view of my own life experience. But it was a hard and enduring process—until that moment when I was diagnosed with cancer.

Here is what happened: instead of bringing me death, cancer brought me life. Yes! You read that correctly. To come alive in life requires learning about who you are and requires understanding the flow of your life as seen through your own eyes and heart. Eventually you may come alive in every cell of your body. Eventually you may begin to experience life to the fullest.

Here's another twist: when all that happens, the fact of death itself becomes meaningless. What becomes important is whether or not you die *healed*.

When I was diagnosed with cancer, I set out on a journey to discover what it means to truly heal. I hoped I would find out. I believed I needed to start by trying to heal my spirit—which felt broken. Eventually, a PET scan would reveal I was cancer free, although the bump in my breast never disappeared.

During my cancer treatments, many people said to me, "You have to write a book about what you are doing." After a while that statement changed to, "You have something people need to hear. You cannot remain silent. You have to write your story." When I seriously considered writing about my life I felt self-conscious and vulnerable. But, as time went by, and I began to change day by day, I realized I needed to open my life and my soul to the world.

As I began to heal, I began to break all my old patterns to the point that I decided to share my experience with you. I began to write in earnest. Once I made the first move to write, the Universe stepped in and helped me in ways I would not have been able to imagine. Not only did I end up writing a book, but, miraculously I received a tree and a baby as well. I am Spanish after all. A child, a book and a tree is my birthright, my cultural heritage. Now it is my legacy.

Learning to love—and to heal—required taking a risk. I would have to change—which meant I would have to take a leap of faith. I did. And what I learned is that we may not be required to jump—ultimately—but if we have to do so, God will be there to catch us.

1

MY JOURNEY BEGINS

I will start from the very beginning. I decided to take on a body. I believe I chose my parents for a specific reason: I knew I needed to learn from the circumstances my parents, my family, my culture and my country had to offer. I needed this experience for my soul to grow. In this lifetime I needed to learn about the power of illness as a teacher. I needed to learn how to heal.

My parents married late in life. I was born when they were almost forty years old. Before I was born, there was an older sister who died at birth. My mother had great difficulty giving birth to my sister, and, of course, this was over sixty years ago when they did not have the advancements in medicine that exist today. She did not dilate and the bag of waters had already broken, so it was too late for a Cesarean. My stillborn sister was a breech delivery.

I always have felt a deep connection to my sister's birth. I have even thought my soul might have been in my sister's body and that possibly, in my sister's body, I was so afraid of what I would have to go through in this lifetime, the possibility of a devastating illness, that I decided not to be born at all—not yet, anyway.

Three months later, my mother became pregnant again—with me—and my parents decided to give birth at a different hospital. Somewhere in their minds was the thought that maybe the doctors had made a mistake or did not have enough knowledge about my mother's condition during the delivery which is why the first baby died. But the hospital wanted my mother to come back. One day, when my mother answered the door, she was surprised to find the director of the hospital standing there. She had come to our house to ask my mother to please have the next baby with them. She explained to my mother that the previous birth was a difficult and unusual case. They had not been prepared for this condition, but now they knew what the problem was. She said the only way for mother and baby to live through another delivery was to go back to the same hospital with the same doctors. She convinced her that the hospital was now prepared for a successful delivery. My mother decided to go back. In the meantime, my mother had morning sickness throughout her pregnancy with me. I remember her telling me that she was still vomiting even during the week she spent in the hospital before the delivery.

The nurses, taking turns, massaged my mother's vagina to try to initiate the dilation process. This went on for several days. My mother was humiliated.

I was born on a Sunday evening. I, too, was almost a breech birth, but in the last moment before being born, I turned around. It seems that this time I was determined to go ahead with my life. A very important soccer game took place that day, and the attention of the hospital staff had to be on my delivery instead of the game. From the start, as my mother would point out to me repeatedly, I came in disrupting other peoples' priorities. I came in disrupting my mother's life and, what's more, the doctors told her never to get pregnant again because she and the child would die. There would be no more children.

My mother told me the story of my birth many times, and each time, I could feel the negative impact my birth had had on her. Every time she found out that someone she knew was pregnant, the expression that came from her heart and out of her mouth was "Poor woman!"

The first day they took me out of the house, probably a week or so after my birth, was to attend a Thanksgiving Mass at the chapel of the hospital. This Mass was ordered by the director and the staff to celebrate the fact of my being alive. Years later, I found out that the chaplain of the hospital who celebrated that Mass was my high school religion teacher who lived near my house. We took the underground to school together and I remember getting along very well with him.

I was baptized just over two weeks after I was born—on the same day of my sister's birth and death, exactly one year later.

My Fluttering Heart

As time passed, my parents began to notice that something was wrong with me. I got sick all the time. The doctors did not know what was wrong; they just knew that, at times, my heart was beating way too fast. Over and over I would fall on my bed and lie there hour after hour without being able to move—just feeling the intense fluttering of my heart. Ultimately, the doctors arrived at the conclusion that my heart was too big. (Later, my husband would often use the expression "big heart" to describe me, and I always was astonished about the connection between the two: the physical heart the doctors described and the spiritual heart my husband referred to). Unfortunately, the doctors could not offer any permanent solution to the chronic heart problem that was destroying my childhood. Their advice was to relax and just try to get through the episodes. Their advice was to manage the best way I could. Really, I could not do anything other than try to manage, and every time I had an episode, I felt the life force leaving me.

I remember as a little girl feeling sick and exhausted and telling my mother "Mamá, I am sick and am going to bed." She would make me a cup of chamomile tea and I would lie in bed hour after hour asking the Virgin Mary to make me well. Then, suddenly I would feel well. I would get up from bed and say: "Mamá, I am well again." These episodes would happen several times a month, and little by little, I came to accept them as a normal part of my daily life. I learned to live facing death.

For the first three years of my life, we lived near El Retiro, the main park in Madrid. At that time, there was a zoo in the park. My mother took me there almost every day. This is the first memory I have about going to the zoo: we would pass by the polar bear cave; I would peek at him through the corner of my eye, and then we would go straight to the elephant's cage. This was our routine and it was impossible for her to get me to see any other animals. I just wanted to stay by the elephant cage all the time. I used to call him *"Feo, feo, feo"* ("Ugly, ugly, ugly"). It seems that that ugliness—the ugliness I saw in the elephant—attracted me. One day after I called him Ugly so many times, he seemed to get tired of it. He disappeared inside his cage. He filled his trunk with water and came back outside to thoroughly soak my mother and me. But I never blamed the elephant and never stopped going back. (By the way, elephants became my favorite animal. In Hindu philosophy, as it turns out, elephants are the beings who remove obstacles and Ganesh, the Hindu elephant god, is my favorite god.)

By the time I started school, the doctors and my parents realized that I got sick whenever I jumped, ran, or became excited. And, I remember very clearly the teacher always coming next to me, just before the bell rang for recess, grabbing my hand before I started to run to the playground with the other kids and taking me to the teachers' room. I spent the recess break in the teachers' room sitting alone in a cramped corner. I became isolated. In some way, this made me different. In some way, this made me ugly—like the elephant.

As in school, I did not have children to play with at home either. I was an only child surrounded by elderly people. The cousins my age all lived in other towns. I saw them only for a few days once a year when all the grandchildren went to spend the holidays in my grandparents' village. Those visits were the highlight of my childhood. This was the only time I had the chance to laugh and play games with children my own age. It was not so important how much playing I could do; it was just the fun of being together all day long.

Most of my childhood I was alone. I sat on the floor playing with quiet toys like paper dolls and reading children's books. I very often said to my mother, "Mamá, I am bored." I did not know the word "depression'" at that time, but I know now that is what I felt. I was not enthusiastic about life. Still, there were isolated moments when I remember having a vivid desire or determination to read a book I had about an octopus. I was attracted to the strangeness of this animal that had black and white stripes. I used to say: "When I have a child, it will be black and white; it will be made of stripes. Mine will not be an ordinary child."

The black and white octopus was not normal. And, I was not a normal girl.

Little by little, I began to understand what I could do—what was possible for a girl who was not normal. I always had to think about how to avoid getting sick.

Children can be the loveliest and cruelest beings. This is because they are honest and they express themselves from their hearts. You always hear the truth from a child. I experienced this each time I had to refuse to play. Sometimes the children got so annoyed with me they pushed me, and of course, right in that moment, my rapid heartbeats would begin. I would get so sick I had to be taken home from school.

To please the children, and to try to make friends, I found a way to join in play by just holding the jump rope while the other kids jumped. This was the only way I could participate.

This was not a very fun life for a child.

My Little Lamb

I spent all my summers in my grandmother's village. My uncle was a shepherd there. Sheep have their lambs in winter and normally these lambs were sold. It was a tradition that one special lamb would be chosen to be killed at the village festivities on the Saint's Day. This lamb would provide a special celebratory meal. It was the only time of the year the people of the village ate lamb.

All the cities and villages in Spain have a patron saint that they celebrate on that Saint's Day. They celebrate with religious ceremonies such as Masses and Processions where they carry the Saint through the main streets of the village. There is special food. There are bullfights. The celebration and dancing last for two or three days and sometimes even longer, depending on the importance of the town. The Saint of my grandmother's village was The Virgin of Neguillan. Her Saint's Day was September 8.

I was really happy to be with the "saved" lamb all summer long. He became my closest friend. I took my naps with him in the back room instead of in a bed. We became absolutely inseparable. I adored him and he adored me. We had a special connection.

One day my grandmother, aunt and uncle sent me to play at a friend's house at the other end of the village. When I came back to my grandmother's home, I found my lamb hanging from the ceiling in the back room. My lamb was dead. They had slit his throat.

The day I found my lamb dead I decided not to eat meat for the rest of my life.

That day, because I refused to eat my lamb, my grandmother cooked French fries and fried eggs for me. She did so every year thereafter during the village festivities.

The Death of My Uncle

When I was seven years old, I made my First Communion in May but there would be no celebration. A few months earlier, death intervened again. My uncle, my mother's brother, lived near us. Every Sunday morning, all my life, he had picked me up and taken me to the park. I always carried a little basket with me. The highlight was to cut a flower and bring it home in the basket. On February 7 of that year, my uncle collapsed at work and died. There would be no First Communion celebration and no more Sunday morning outings. We were in mourning.

My uncle died on February 7. Later, when I began to study Recall Healing with Dr. Gilbert Renaud (the study of the emotional trauma behind conditions and behaviors), I realized February 7 was a critical recurring date in my life. I will talk about this date more later.

Gradually, my frustration with life grew more and more intense. I remember getting angry and asking my mother: "Why did you bring me here?" I would yell, "I do not like it here. I do not like this planet. I did not ask you to bring me here! I wish I had never been born!" As I grew older, I realized how much pain that must have caused my mother. When my anger was not so extreme, I started containing myself and not saying this out loud—even though I still felt this way in my heart

.

2

DREAMS SHATTERED

I was born in December, which meant that by law I could start school at a younger age if the school gave permission. I was allowed to enter school at age three. I completed my elementary school studies early at age nine.

Soon after that school year began, each student was required to have a medical check-up. My results were bad. It was my heart. From that day on, I was excused from all the exercise classes. I could either spend time studying alone in the classroom or come to school later or leave earlier. Those were my options. My mother was called in to talk to the school doctor about my health. When I was sitting with my mother in the doctor's office, the doctor said to my mother: "She will never be able to have children of her own. Your daughter's heart is so bad she will never be able to survive the delivery of a baby."

Also, there were exciting day trips at school I could never go on because they always involved too much walking or hiking and neither my parents nor the school wanted me to get sick. As I moved into puberty, my rapid heartbeat episodes became less frequent. I got to know my body better and was able to control more of what I was able to do. Also, many times it seemed like there was absolutely no reason for me to have these rapid heartbeat episodes. They would just come out of the blue. This happened over and over and over—until I had open heart surgery.

Relationship with my Parents

I never had a good relationship with my mother. We both had a very strong personality and most of the time we did not view life in the same way. Later, I was told that the relationship between a mother and child gets established during childbirth—depending on what they both go through in that moment. In my case, this makes perfect sense because of my mother's difficult pregnancy and the struggle we both went through during delivery. Both of us were face-to-face with death. That struggle remained with us the rest of our lives together.

My father held two jobs. I got along well with my father, but he was hardly at home except to eat and sleep. He had one morning off each week. That day he took me out to museums, churches and other places where he shared his love of art with me.

He took pride in his clothes too, and the way he looked. As I grew up, we used to go shopping for his clothes together, so between the two of us, we chose the proper attire. I learned to develop my sense of color and fashion from him. I always felt close to my father and removed from my mother. My father was a very religious person who liked to go to church. My mother was not religious at all and going to church on Sundays was just a social event for her. I had my First Communion and Confirmation because it was part of the school program and the thing to do, but not because of any religious meaning that was taught at home. In fact, I always went to public schools because they were cheaper than Catholic schools, and that fit into my mother's values of spending the least amount of money on education. My mother came from a very poor family and her father died when she was seven years old. As the oldest of five children, when her father died she had to take over his job as a shepherd to help my grandmother support the family, so she never learned how to read or write.

As a child, I could not understand why I was denied so many essentials in education. It was not until I was in my twenties that I could relate my mother's life to my own and understand clearly why my mother behaved this way about my education. Since she never praised me for getting good grades, I learned to rely on my father for encouragement. He was the one who spent time every year putting protective covers, labels and titles on my books so I would feel proud when I went to school.

Even as my love for art was just beginning, it was ended at almost the same time. At age twelve, I was sexually abused by an artist—in my own home. This blocked me from appreciating art for many years. Looking at paintings reminded me of the abuse. As I grew up, I realized I had to overcome this obstacle. I had always loved art—like I loved my father—and I wanted art to be a large part of my life. When I was in my late twenties I started going to art museums again. This was hard in the beginning but my love of art had been—and would be again—deeply important in my life.

Later, when I studied Recall Healing, I found out why I would be able to overcome the damage from this incident. Recall Healing teaches that if something is in your conscious memory you can overcome it. If a memory is subconscious it is almost impossible to overcome. I could overcome the sexual abuse and its connection with art because all this was in my conscious memory; I was all too familiar with the details. However, I was not able to overcome another aspect of the sexual abuse. Why? Because it was not in my conscious memory; it was in my unconscious memory. Working with Gilbert Renaud I realized that my mother, who was the protector of me and the house, was ultimately responsible for this abuse because it took place within the sanctuary of our home. Recall Healing states that whatever abides in your unconscious memory can turn into illness. It is only when it becomes conscious that we can begin to heal. When I became conscious of my mother's role in this incident I could begin to heal this part of my relationship with her. I also realized that because of the strong and positive relationship I had with my father my relationship with men in general was not damaged by the sexual abuse. Ironically, it was my relationship with art which suffered the most.

Teenage Years

When I was thirteen years old, I put on a lot of weight during the summer, and it seemed like my metabolism had stopped working normally. So I started going to doctors to control it. At that time, going to the doctor to check your metabolism was quite an ordeal. I had to arrive at the doctor's office a couple of hours early for a test. I had to sit uncomfortably without moving in a recliner chair—way too big for my size. For the test they put a clothespin on my nose to prevent me from breathing. Then I had to go back the next day to pick up the test results. The doctor put me on a very severe diet to lose the weight I had gained. At that time, saccharine was the only sugar substitute and many times I forgot to carry it with me which is how I got used to going without sweeteners in my drinks. Also about that time, I needed to take vitamins and the doctor decided to give me ones that tasted like Coca-Cola so it would be easier for me to take them. At the end of a few months of taking those vitamins I could not bear the taste of Coca-Cola or any other kind of soft drink.

So the Universe took care of my diet at a very early stage in life.

By age fifteen, I had finished high school. I was very clear about what I wanted to do next: I wanted to go to the university and study political science. However, my mother's plans for me were quite different.

When I finished high school and told my mother I wanted to continue my education and go to the university, she simply said *No*. My friend's older sister, who tutored us in mathematics, even came to my house to try to convince my mother to let me go to the university since I wouldn't be able to work legally at age fifteen, anyway. But there was no way to convince her. She said we had no money, but that was not true. The university where I wanted to go was in my town and was a state school that anyone could afford. That didn't matter. My mother said I wasn't going and no one would change her mind. My father was not much help since my mother ruled the house with an iron hand. We had to abide by her laws, no matter what. On reflection, I realize this was the reason my father was very happy having two jobs and being at home as little as possible.

My mother was adamant. She told me since I would "marry and have children"—even though that was impossible—I did not need to continue studying. In the very moment when my mother said, "You will marry and have children," I vowed to myself to never get married and definitely to never have children. I decided consciously to go through life without leaving anything behind. I vowed I would never have a child, never write a book and certainly not plant a tree. At that time I was not even thinking about the fact that I was physically unable to have children because of my heart.

Years later when I studied Recall Healing, I realized that my mother's statement that I should marry and have children registered in my subconscious mind as her wish for me to die. My subconscious, not my conscious mind, made this association from the "you'll die in childbirth" conversation we had with the school doctor when I was nine years old.

Instead of going to the university then, I spent the next year studying shorthand, typing and bookkeeping to become a secretary. It was easy work. And it was boring. I had free time, and I was lucky that there were a lot of books in my house to read—even though my mother couldn't read. We had inherited the entire library of a professor, which included the great classics authors, such as Shakespeare and Cervantes and the most relevant works of Spanish literature. I read every book in the house.

By age sixteen, I finished my secretarial studies, and since I was still too young to work, I began studies at a private academy to prepare me for a job with the State. That was a good alternative to going to the university. At that time everyone in Spain aspired to work for the government or in official positions with major banks or large companies that had strong ties with the government. These jobs offered many advantages such as short working hours, good health and retirement benefits and plenty of vacation time plus the ultimate in job security with a guarantee of never losing your job. You had to study and pass a difficult entry exam to get these jobs, and there was a lot of competition. When I was prepared, I took the exam and passed. I was so happy! I was not going to get a university degree but at least I would get one of those highly prized jobs.

In my excitement, I forgot I was required to pass a medical exam before actually getting the job, and of course when the results came back, they told me I was disqualified for the position because of my heart. The Director of the Academy that had prepared me for the government exam called me into his office and told me that I was wasting my time because I would never get one of those jobs anyway. He said, "Just accept it and get a job in the private sector." If they ever gave me a medical exam in the private sector, it would be after I was already working and it would be too late to rescind the job offer.

As my dreams were shattered one by one, my energy began to diminish and my hope began to fade. Over time I began to live like the living dead. Ultimately I lived biding my time until I would leave this planet.

I did date boys my age, but the moment I felt more interest than just a friendship on their part or mine, I would cut off the relationship before letting it go any further, thus causing a more painful separation. There was only one time that I had a boyfriend that lasted for more than a few months. I broke it off when I remembered, completely and totally, I would never be able to have a child.

Marriage was not completely out of my future, but being a mother was. I think a woman always imagines the beauty of being the mother of a small child, but to me the idea of experiencing my baby's childhood seemed horrendous. How could I bring anyone into this world considering my own experience—even if I had the physical capacity to do so? I had so many bad memories of my growing up years, and I was so unhappy about the fact of being alive, that I could not imagine being so unfair as to bring anyone into this world.

As such, I learned to live a life without dreams. Even by the end of my teenage years, due to my poor health and my mother's narrow concept of life, my dreams were already drying up.

It was in this mood of despair I started working for a private company. I was nineteen years old. After I had worked there for a few months, I realized I needed to speak at least one or two foreign languages to get a better job as a secretary in the private sector. By this time, I had met an English girl while on vacation on the coast of Spain, and I decided to go to her hometown in England to work as an *au pair* to improve my English.

My ability to read and write English was quite good, but I needed to practice speaking to become fluent.

As it turned out, moving to England would become the first step of my going into the convent. And, going into the convent would be the first step in my conscious search for a spiritual life.

Angels in My Journey

I went to Bournemouth, a town on the south coast. My friend and her parents lived there and my parents were happy I had a family to care for me while I was in England.

When I first arrived in England I got a job as an *au pair* with a family with two small children. This situation was really hard for me because I had never been around children and did not know how to deal with them. After two months, the family had to move to another town, forcing me to find yet another family. The next family that hired me had two teenage daughters who were studying abroad. This turn of events appeared to be a clear intervention from the Universe.

The new family was quite wealthy and, because they had a maid, my only duties were light housekeeping. They made sure that our schedules did not conflict so that I would be home when they were gone. Their main objective in having an *au pair* was to be sure that there was always someone in the house. The family was Jewish, and I was happy to have the chance to learn about their religion and lifestyle. They made me feel like part of the family and included me in their Jewish traditions and ceremonies.

They were pleasantly surprised that it felt so natural for me to participate with them. Since my last name was a Jewish name,

Chacobo (Jacob), they concluded that I was Jewish by ancestry, even though I was raised a Catholic. This made sense to me since many Jews remained in Spain during the Inquisition and were required to become Catholic. I have always had a fascination about my heritage and was open to the experience and eager to learn about Judaism. This family turned out to be the perfect match for me.

At the time most *au pairs* in England were students. I was studying English to prepare for the Cambridge Exam, a certificate in the English Language. At the school I attended, I met three nuns who lived in a convent near the house of this Jewish family where I lived and worked.

I became very good friends with one of the nuns. She was six years older than me. We studied together at the convent which happened to be walking distance from my house. As our friendship developed, I started to learn about religious life. Another spiritual dimension began to open.

My First Try: Entering the Convent

When I came back to Spain, I started going to meetings for secular youth organized by the Handmaids of the Sacred Heart—the nuns I met in England. This is the time I began to consider going into religious life. Ultimately, I found a spiritual director who was a Jesuit priest. It happened that he was very close to the cloistered branch of the Carmelite Order, *Carmelitas Descalzas* (Discalced Carmelites).

I was never thrilled about becoming a teacher, which is what most of the nuns did in the Handmaids of the Sacred Heart Order, but I was delighted with the prospect of spending my life as a cloistered nun. As a cloistered nun I would be alone in a cell without contact with the outside world.

My desire to live a cloistered life was not because the doctor told my mother and me that I should not attempt to have a child. Rather, it was because I had vowed not to give in to my mother's wishes of getting married and having children.

If I became a cloistered nun, I could help all humanity by spending my life in prayer. As well as being closer to God and Spirit and far away from what I considered "Life," this really appealed to me. Also my health would not be a problem there; my life would be limited to living in one convent without having to face missionary work or travel to distant places. The convent seemed ideal.

When I told my parents about my plans, my mother immediately said *No*. Even though I was twenty three years old and did not need her consent, she forbade me from leaving the house. She said I only could go out to go to work. My father said nothing. One of my aunts, however, who was the widow of my uncle who died when I was seven years old, knew my wishes and came to help me. She encouraged me to give notice at work without telling my parents—which I did. Then I left the house.

I chose a convent in the country, in the province of Avila, about two hours by car from Madrid. It was a branch of the cloistered Carmelites that had split away from the regular Order in order to retain the customs that were in place during the time of the reformer St. Theresa of Jesus. This particular branch of Discalced Carmelites lived very much like the nuns did in the Sixteenth Century. They were vegetarians. They wore a habit that weighed twenty-two pounds all year round. They had no hot water or bathroom, although they did have toilets. They broke the ice on winter mornings to wash themselves, and they abided by the rules of silence. They did not talk to anyone. As a result, they did not establish personal relationships. They were allowed to talk two hours a day, one hour after lunch and one hour after dinner, in a general conversation directed by the Mother Prioress. This isolation and austerity appealed to me deeply. For the first time in my life I felt like a fish in water. But this feeling did not last long.

The Mother Prioress was transferred after I had been in the convent for only two months. Her replacement was someone I never got along with. We just could not understand each other, although I must say, we really tried our best to communicate. In this branch of the Carmelites, we were not allowed to have a spiritual director other than the Mother Prioress. Therefore, I did not have anyone to talk to about my spiritual life, my anxieties, my worries or even my happiness.

We spent many hours in prayer and meditation, although we never had formal training about how to meditate. Many times I would fall asleep during meditation because I was too tired from not getting enough sleep at night. The thirty minutes assigned to us for reading was right after nap time, and nap time was only half an hour, so just when I started to fall asleep, it was time to wake up and start my reading. At this point, I was so sleepy I never got much reading done. Not being able to feed myself spiritually with readings and not being able to communicate with the Mother Prioress started taking its toll on me. I felt drained spiritually. Gradually I began to feel more and more confined by not being able to deepen my spiritual life.

There was a rapid progression in the different stages of training. We were postulants for six months, novices for one year, afterwards making the temporal vows. Then the perpetual vows were made four years later. By the time I made my temporal vows, I had serious doubts about whether living as a nun was my true calling in life. The Mother Prioress knew that I was having these thoughts, but after much discussion and evaluation, we both agreed that God's plans were above ours and I made my temporal vows. I remember crying so hard during the ceremony. I felt as if I were being slaughtered—just like the pet lamb of my childhood. It was February 7 when I made my vows—the same date that my uncle died when I was seven years old.

Families were only allowed to visit the nuns in the convent once a month, and even then there was no personal contact. We saw our families only through the iron grille on the window. In my case, this was not an issue at all because I never heard from my parents during this time. Due to my special circumstances of being an only child and having escaped from my house to enter the convent, I was allowed, with a special permit, to write to my parents every week. I wrote faithfully the whole time I was there. We all hoped that with time, my parents would renew their relationship with me and come to the convent to visit. They finally did but the circumstances under which they came would prove to be quite different.

After a year-and-a-half in the convent the situation had not improved. I was feeling increasingly lost spiritually. Finally, I decided that to be true to myself, I needed to leave. When I wrote the weekly letter to my parents, I told them I would be leaving the convent soon and that they did not have to worry because I had already made all the arrangements to live in a religious residence. I would find a job and restart my life. This was the only time I received a reply. My mother called the convent and said they were coming to pick me up the following Sunday. This added stress in the following days because the Mother Prioress wanted me to leave with my parents, but the Religious Vicar, who had to sign the annulment of my vows before I could leave, was away and could not do it. It was a relief when he returned Saturday night at midnight. He signed the vows annulment and called the convent at midnight to authorize my release.

When I look back at that time of my life, I can see that I

made the right decision to go to the convent, but not for the right reasons. It is true that I was on a spiritual quest, but at the time, I did not know there was any other way other than to enter a convent. What appealed to me the most was the desire to withdraw from the world rather than the vocation to serve others. A life of solitude, being far away from my family, my job and the world in general where I never really felt comfortable, is what attracted me more than my desire to give my life to God in this way. I realized I had made this decision by a process of elimination, and for the wrong reasons, even though my intentions were positive.

Many people thought I had lost two years of my life in the convent, but I never felt that was true. I gained a broader perspective over the years of just how fruitful that time was, and how much that experience helped me in life, especially in the treatment I chose to follow when diagnosed with cancer. The nuns gave me a new perspective on life, and they taught me the discipline required for a spiritual commitment that has served me well. It was like attending school with an excellent training for life that the average person will never have. When I visited Thailand, and saw all those young men serving as monks standing on the side of the road and depending on others for food for the day, I thought to myself, "What an excellent training!" I used to tease my husband by saying to him "Thank God I have been a nun, if not, I would have divorced you already." That is how I feel about those years in the convent. Wearing the same twenty-two pound habit day after day, not having bathrooms and experiencing hardships in general turned out to be not so important. What turned out to be important for me was the realization that spiritual growth is what matters most. There is a bigger and more profound perspective to life that living in the convent made me realize.

Back To Regular Life

When I arrived back home, there was very little of mine left in the house or in my room. It was as though I had never existed. I also noticed that my mother had gotten rid of most of the religious figures that were in the house. All the crosses and religious statues had disappeared. The only thing left of mine was the Dumbo the Elephant poster on the wall in front of my bed. Everything was gone—but my connection to the elephant remained: *Feo, Feo, Feo,* I thought.

The convent was never mentioned again and my parents acted as if those two years had never existed. Not to talk about my experience was like an undisclosed agreement among all of us.

I needed to wear a wig because we had our heads shaved in the convent. Also, I needed to learn to walk with shoes again. After two years of walking in sandals (*espadrilles*) made of straw (*esparto*), it took some adjustment to get my feet back in shoes.

Since it was the beginning of summer, we all decided it would be best for me to go to the beach in the northwest part of Spain where my father's two elderly cousins owned a hotel and apartments that they rented during the summer. The idea was that I could help them out with the business while my hair grew back and I got used to normal life again.

I came back to Madrid at the end of September. I started to look for a job. On November 20, 1975, I started working as the secretary to the editor of a newspaper in Madrid. I remember the date so distinctly because it was the day Franco died and there was a special frenzy in the newsroom.

I loved my job, and even though I worked half a day, I still received full pay. The editor had two secretaries, one for the morning and one for the evening. I was the morning secretary and my job was mainly to organize the public relations agenda for my boss, which gave me the opportunity to meet many interesting people.

As I finished work early in the afternoon, I still had half a day off, so I started to study political science at the university in the afternoon and evening. I also began to study German at the Goethe Institute. It did not take me long to realize that my health did not allow me to do what I wanted, so I enrolled in correspondence courses to continue my education. Although the correspondence university did not offer the degree I wanted, I had to mentally adjust to what was available. After two years of trying this approach, I realized I had to give up the idea of having a university degree. I decided to study German and nothing else. By then I regularly went to Germany on vacation to improve my language skills as best as I could.

As I always said, God gave me the job I could handle. Because of my heart condition I had never had much stamina and tired very easily. After coming home from work for lunch in the mid-afternoon, I always needed to have a nap after my meal. I had to pace myself during the day—which still continues.

3

MY FIRST DECISION TO "LIVE"

Two years later, when I was twenty-seven years old, the newspaper decided to provide a medical checkup for all their employees. For the first time ever, the doctors were able to define the problem with my heart. They diagnosed me with Wolf Parkinson White Syndrome which means there is an extra energy channel in the heart. When the energy shifted into the extra channel, it would cause my heart to beat between 350 and 400 beats per minute, not the normal 60 to 80 beats per minute. The doctors explained that I could die at any moment when this happens, because the heart is not designed to beat at such high speeds. They were really surprised that I had been able to go through these episodes throughout my life without any major consequence. They told me to go to the nearest hospital whenever this happened again, and that is when I started my "peregrination" through different Intensive Care Units (ICUs) where I would spend two or three days at a time.

After a few hours in the hospital, I would let the nurses know I was feeling better and ready to go home. They explained that even though my heart was beating at 120 or 150 beats per minute, and I was feeling better in comparison to how I had felt before, I was not well yet and needed to remain in the hospital until my heart was beating normally. They did not really do anything for me, but they wanted to keep me under observation. If my heart stopped, they would be able to resuscitate me. That was the only reason for me being hospitalized in the ICU.

In spite of all this drama, I was always able to look at the humorous side. Every time I arrived at the hospital reception area and let them know I was sick and needed to be admitted to the ICU, the staff would inevitably look at me with a strange expression. It was as though they were thinking that what I really needed was to be admitted to a psychiatric hospital. This only lasted however until they called the doctor in charge and listened to my heart. Then a big commotion would start. They would not even allow me to move and would take me on a gurney from the hospital reception area to the ICU.

Eventually, there was a specific medicine from Switzerland that the doctors hoped could help me with my heart problem, but the long-term side effects were not known. They said I could very well die from taking it. After being on this medication for a while, the doctors and I agreed it was not worth the risk, so I stopped taking the pills. By then, I was told that the surgery I needed was only performed in Paris, Amsterdam and the United States. They said they could not do anything more for me in Spain—except to continue monitoring me in the ICU during these episodes.

Sometimes the episodes became so intense that when the rapid heartbeats began, I lost my eyesight for a few seconds. This happened once while I was driving. There was a traffic jam, and my friend who was in the car with me was able to take the wheel while I put on the brakes. She was able to maneuver the car to the side of the road. This frightening incident made me realize how dangerous it was to live like this. If I had been alone in the car and driving at a regular speed, I might have killed myself—which did not make much difference to me—but more importantly, I could have caused an accident that could have killed someone else. The thought of being responsible for someone else's death really mattered to me. This experience impacted me so strongly I started to think seriously about having open-heart surgery.

I did not know anyone in Amsterdam or Paris at that time, and I did not speak Dutch or French, but I did speak English and had several friends in the United States. So I decided to go to the United States on vacation and travel to California, Florida, Pennsylvania and Washington, D.C., where my friends lived, to investigate the available options for my surgery.

At the time, I had a friend living in Menlo Park, California and she arranged for a consultation at Stanford University Medical Center. The head of the Cardiology Department immediately sent me to the proper specialist, and without any hesitation, the doctor offered to perform the surgery for free. I would only have to find a way to pay for the hospital charges. I remember him asking me, "How did you know I was here?" At the time I really did not know why he asked me that, but now I know that the Universe guided me in the right direction.

After visiting California, I left for Miami to visit a friend and then traveled on to Philadelphia to meet with another friend, the nun I had met in England ten years earlier. She had been the strongest influence on my decision to enter the convent. She took it into her own hands to find a way for me to pay for the hospital charges at Stanford.

We went to Washington DC. We talked to Senator Cranston's aide who told us there were grants given regularly at Stanford, and he would let us know when they came up and when to apply for them. Sure enough, two months later, he contacted my friend, the nun. She contacted me and then I contacted my friend in Menlo Park who applied for the grant in my name. Two months after applying, I had open-heart surgery at Stanford University Medical Center in February. I only had to pay a total of $3,000 for my surgery which covered the anesthesiologist's and radiologist's bills. It seems ironic that when I was a foreigner, I was able to have surgery and stay in the hospital for free, and then when I became a U.S. citizen, I could not get health insurance because I had a pre-existing condition—but that is another story.

The day before the surgery, I was worried because I could see that everyone who was having surgery the following day was visited by the doctors and given explanations about their procedures— everyone except me. Finally at ten o'clock on the night before surgery, one of the doctors came to explain to me that the primary doctor performing my surgery, the one I met in my first consultation at Stanford, had flown in from Hawaii that day and they were busy explaining my tests to him. I was going to be only the sixth person operated on at Stanford for this illness. They discovered that the extra energy channel and the normal channel were so close together that the fast heartbeats were probably caused when the energy went to both channels. The doctors considered freezing one of the channels, but this involved microscopic surgery and they were concerned that if they closed them too much, I would have to have a pacemaker installed.

I thought it was going to be too complicated to go back to Spain with a pacemaker, and then be required to have follow-up in Spain. This was a good excuse to prepare to die and not have to go through this "complication." When my closest friend found out I was contemplating death—knowing me and my lack of interest in life—she said, "I am not going to hang up the phone until you tell me that you want to live, regardless of the outcome of the surgery, whether you end up with a pacemaker or not." At that time, international calls were expensive and to be on the phone for a long time was costly. In the end, the call was worth the price. It took me a while to say *yes* to life, but I finally did.

After the surgery, I was left with the installation setup for a pacemaker, but after having some tests a few days later, they found out it was not going to be needed. This was such a relief to me. Since I did not have family in the U.S., and because my friend who lived locally did not really have time to take care of me due to her work and study schedule, the doctors decided to keep me in the hospital for three weeks. Because they were so impressed with how well I spoke English, they used my skills as a translator.

The doctors would call me into different patients' rooms to translate for them, which kept me occupied and helped me to get through the long hospital days. I think I found this work really difficult to do because it forced me to look at life and death again, not only my own, but others.'

When I was discharged from the hospital, my close friend, the same one who kept me on the phone the night before my surgery, came to live with me. She took care of me for a month until we were able to return to Spain.

For years my mother kept a little yellow canary in a cage. The bird had stopped singing the day I left for my surgery. When I arrived back home she started to sing again. Everyone noticed the coincidence.

When I was discharged from the hospital, I was told that I had a heart murmur. Later, we found out I had a hole in my heart. Looking at this metaphorically, it makes total sense: I had always felt I had a hole in my life.

My heart has been the most delicate part of my body, and when I am under stress, my heart literally skips many beats at a time. So, I do not think it is strange that I have developed a special relationship with my physical heart, and, over time, a special appreciation for it keeping me alive all these years. I am really aware of my heart. I treat my heart like I would a friend and I protect my heart fiercely. For example, if a doctor prescribes a heart medication that I have a hunch might harm my heart, I absolutely refuse to take it.

Even though I had a hole in my life my precious heart kept me alive so I could continue my journey until I got cancer—and I could learn how to really heal.

4

A NEW BEGINNING

I remember commenting to my friends, "If I marry, I will marry an older man. I want someone who has had children already and will not ask me to have any." Also, I always had difficulty interacting with people my own age because of my physical limitations. I never had the same strength or stamina as others my age and my friends always had to adapt to my pace: walking slowly with me, letting a bus go by because I was unable to run to catch it, and generally limiting themselves by going to plays or movies rather than enjoying outdoor activities. As such, I always felt that a man my age was never going to be able to yield to my needs or make accommodations to adapt to my lifestyle, whereas a slower pace would be natural for an older person.

My Wedding

In May of 1983, one year after my heart surgery, when I arrived home after work my mother told me, "Someone has called asking for you but he cannot speak Spanish and I do not know who he is." Then he called again and the same thing happened. Finally

31

someone who spoke Spanish called and my mother told him the proper time to call—when I would be home.

That is the first contact I had with Bob, the man who would become my husband. We had a mutual friend, Maggie, who was an elderly woman I met through the friend I stayed with when I had surgery at Stanford. She shared the same surname as Bob. Because they were both Shermans, they became instant friends when they met in a class. When Maggie found out that Bob was coming to Europe, she gave him my phone number and asked him to contact me while he was in Madrid visiting friends. These friends coincidentally lived a few blocks from my house. I remember my father asking me whether I knew what Bob looked like so I would recognize him when I met him. I responded, "Papá, he is American! He will be in tennis shoes and plaid pants—he will be the worst dressed man in the hotel lobby. I will certainly be able to recognize him!"

Well, when I met him, he was wearing a gorgeous beige suit, brown tie and brown shoes. It was love at first sight—and I always said it was the way he was dressed that did it. He always replied that he had sent his plaid pants to the cleaners on that very day. He had such a good sense of humor. Later I found out that he never cared very much about his clothes, and I never really saw him well-dressed again unless I had an influence on the outfit he was going to wear. It seems that the Universe inspired him that day with his choice of clothes because of the impression it was going to have on me, especially when I was expecting him to be so unattractively attired. It was as though the Universe knew we were meant to be together. It was time for me to move to a new country and to expand my worldview. Without knowing it, I was yearning to awaken the dormant parts of myself, and he was the spark that ignited a new sense of aliveness in me.

Falling in love with Bob and moving to America prepared me

with everything I would later need to face cancer in the future by myself. First of all, Bob was very independent with regard to his own medical care. Secondly, moving to America opened my mind and allowed me to begin to satisfy my insatiable thirst for learning. All of this enabled me to become an independent decision-maker.

On our first date, I took Bob sightseeing and then we had dinner together. He had planned to go to Toledo the next day, but had not made any arrangements for the trip. I was quite surprised but thought nothing more about it. After we were married, I discovered this was a common behavior pattern of his—to not make plans.

Since I knew there was not much work to do at the newspaper the next day, and I was interested in getting to know Bob better, I asked my boss for the day off. I drove Bob to Toledo. Because he was a friend of Maggie's, and my parents had met Maggie when she was visiting in Madrid, they asked me to bring him home that night for dinner. My mother was an excellent cook and she made a nice Spanish meal of tapas.

On my way to work the next day, I took him to the airport to continue his three month trip through Europe. Two days later he called from Athens to ask me if I wanted him to change his itinerary and return to Madrid before going back to the States. Of course I said *Yes*.

That was how our relationship started. Although we only had been together in person for three months—and we got to know each other mainly through letters and phone calls—one-and-a-half years later we married. When we married, he was sixty-eight years old and I was thirty-four.

The U.S.A.: Married Life

When my friends found out that I was marrying and moving to live in California, none of them were surprised. On the contrary, they all told me, "We never saw you really identified with Spain and settled here. It is really quite appropriate that you are moving to the United States." And it was true, I never felt entirely comfortable in Spain. In fact, when I moved to San Francisco, I felt completely at home. I did not meet anyone from Spain or speak Spanish for two years after moving to my new country and I did not miss anything from my former life. I was open to a new beginning and I never felt homesick.

In the Spanish culture at that time, children left home either to get married or to take a job in another town. My parents had a mixed reaction to my marriage—which was the opposite of what I would have expected. My mother was very accepting and my father was not happy at all. My mother and I knew how hard it was for us to live together. I had tried to leave home several times without success. On the other hand, my father was heart-broken; he did not want to see me go. Also he and I were allies "against" my mother and he did not want to lose the support I provided. I also think he felt I was abandoning him to take care of another man almost his age. Consistent with his usual pattern, my father did not verbally express his feelings but we both knew what was going on in his heart.

A year after we got married, I was not really interested in going back home to visit my parents, but Bob insisted that we go. He said, "Your parents need to know you are happy." So we went to visit them. My father and my husband did not speak the same language, but, after they spent time together, they formed a close bond. They understood each other well. It was during this visit that my father accepted my husband. It is a common belief that women marry men like their fathers, and, I will say that in my case, it was true. Both my father and Bob were number Nine in the Enneagram and their characters were very similar. I discovered this when I studied the Enneagram a couple of years later. The Enneagram is a personality typing system of nine interconnected personality types. It can be used as a method for self-understanding and self-development. It is often presented as a path to higher states of being. Sure enough, my husband and my father belonged to the same category. They were both accepting, non-judgmental, calm and patient—and they both tended to be procrastinators. As I mentioned, I learned my husband was a number Nine. I know now that this was one reason I fell in love with him. Because of my own Enneagram number, Six, I only had to strive to integrate his qualities to improve myself. As I always strove for learning and improvement, when I learned the Enneagram I realized the Universe had given me the proper partner for my spiritual growth. Certainly, I learned a lot of virtues from him that would help me in my future without him and in my cancer treatments. From Bob I learned patience. He had more patience than anyone I have ever known—even if he did procrastinate.

A couple of years before I met my husband, he had had a heart attack and was told he needed bypass surgery for three clogged arteries. He never had the operation. He spent a month at the Pritikin Longevity Center in Santa Monica. Here, Bob learned to cook nutritious meals and how to exercise and live a healthy lifestyle. The Pritikin Longevity Center was dedicated to healing through diet and exercise.

This new way of living served Bob well for fifteen years until he had a second heart attack. We thought there was no way to avoid having bypass surgery this time. It seemed that the circumstances were forcing us to choose surgery, but deep in our hearts, we were looking for another solution to our "problem." Fortunately, we found the Preventive Medical Center in San Francisco where Bob was able to get chelation therapy. The treatment he received served him for ten years more until he died in 2008 at ninety-two years of age.

It was through this experience with him that I became aware of alternatives to allopathic medicine. I learned there are many ways to define and treat disease. I learned about the wonders of diet and exercise and about how each form of treatment affects your frame of mind. This knowledge became instrumental in the way I chose to treat my cancer.

When Bob and I got married, many people asked me whether it was difficult for me to follow his diet and lifestyle, not realizing that this was already my diet and lifestyle. I did not eat meat. It did wonders for me to stop drinking milk and to eliminate many dairy products from my diet. I never liked to cook very much but I did like baking, so we still had healthy treats.

When we were newly married, we went to exercise classes at a hospital near our home. The classes were structured in a way that gave me great confidence, since I still was afraid of getting sick if I exercised. Bob and I both had a similar energy level, so we were able to keep pace with each other.

After moving to the U.S., I started going to college. The first classes I took were to learn more about the United States and particularly California, and then when I felt I knew the basics about my new country, I started taking Art History, Philosophy, and Religion. I also liked weekend seminars, and I convinced my husband to come along to many of them. That is when I started learning about dream theory and the Enneagram.

My Parents' Death

In my early forties I started having menopausal problems. I was suffering from the depression and lack of interest in life that I had experienced previously. When I was forty-two, my father passed away. This is when I started going to a psychiatrist and asking for antidepressants. It was very comforting to be able to spend time with my father before his passing and to be with him at that moment, but after his death, my relationship with my mother became even worse than it had been before. By then I knew all about the Enneagram personality typing system and her personality number type. This knowledge helped me to understand what was going on for her and the dynamics of our relationship. She was a number Two, and as I learned about the Enneagram, I was able to put her virtues and defects in perspective. She had had a hard life. I was able to begin to understand her compulsive desire to help others as a way to manipulate them. Manipulation was a survival mechanism for her. I began to understand the source of my mother's pride and all the feelings she had beneath the surface; she did not pay attention to her own needs. Finally, I began to understand how her defects became her strengths. These characteristics helped her to overcome her hard childhood and to establish a good life of her own. I began to stop judging her. I could not change her, but I could accept her as she was and concentrate on learning my lessons—because she was the mother I chose.

Without my father, my mother became very insecure and suspicious of everyone. She felt totally disempowered. The tools she had used to survive—which she had used to control my father—no longer applied. As a result, it became necessary for her to look within to find answers. However, she did not know how to do this. At the same time, she was too proud to ask for help. I began to understand her better but I felt incapable of helping her. I knew I was the last person she would accept help from. I could sense her anger towards me because I was not there to help her in the way she wanted, so she withdrew further and further from me. The reality of the situation took a heavy emotional toll on me. I had to leave my mother alone in Spain. Since she did not know how to read or write, life became extremely complicated for her since she lived by herself. Her only support was from one of her younger sisters. This sister had breast cancer and, at that time, was also diagnosed with bone cancer. She was told she was not going to live much longer. Living almost half way around the world, there was nothing I could do for my mother or my aunt.

My mother lived five more years; the last two were spent in a homecare facility because she broke her femur. Due to her severe osteoporosis, the doctor was unable to put pins in her thigh bone; she was not going to be able to walk again. It happened that my husband and I were in Madrid visiting her when she broke her leg. I felt lucky that I could be there throughout the ordeal. I found a homecare facility for her while she was still in the hospital, because I knew she was going to be in a wheelchair for the rest of her life. That is when I learned that death does not always happen at the moment a person stops breathing or when the heart stops beating. Sometimes it happens when we are still alive.

I had to lie to my mother and tell her she was going to the homecare facility temporarily for rehabilitation. Then I told her that as soon as she could walk again, she would be able to go back home. In my heart I knew that she would never go home again, and even though I had the strength to show a calm face to her when we were together, I just could not stop crying when we were apart. Although this was not my mother's actual death, to me it felt like the end.

For two years I went to Spain often to visit her. After a while she stopped recognizing me and other people as well. It seemed to me she actually chose to stop remembering—in that she had not been diagnosed with Alzheimer's disease or dementia. Soon she was no longer able to reason or make sense when she tried to speak. She had always been a very strong woman and it may have been less painful for her to lose her mind than to see herself no longer living in her house; to see herself alone and in a wheelchair.

Bob and I had purchased tickets to visit my mother for a couple of weeks when suddenly I had to take him to the hospital. He had severe back pain. I called my mother's homecare center to let them know we had to cancel the trip because my husband was in the hospital. They informed me that my mother was dying: she was unconscious. Being with her, they said, would be for my own solace. She would not know whether I was there or not. They encouraged me to stay home and take care of my husband.

After a few days of tests, we were told that my husband had a fractured vertebra. When everything was arranged for him, I would be able to leave for Spain. I bought my plane ticket, but the day before I was supposed to leave I received a phone call letting me know my mother had passed away.

In Spain, the dead are buried within twenty-four hours and, since I was her only family, the funeral home agreed to keep her body for burial until I arrived. Not even one tear came out of my eyes. My mother had died to me two years earlier and I had already spent two years grieving. The actual burial was just a ritual I had to go through. Coincidentally, my mother died on the day of St. Therese of Jesus, the patron saint of the religious order where I was a nun. My mother had been so against my going into the convent. That was because she expected me to take care of her in her old age. As it turned out, even though I was no longer a nun, she was alone in the last days of her life. She was alone when she passed away.

After my mother died, I moved everything out of my house

in Spain. I wanted to put it on the rental market. My husband was getting old and it was a long trip, so I knew we were not going to be traveling there many more times.

Many people have asked me over the years how I was able to make so many drastic changes, how I could cut ties so easily, and leave everything behind. Making big decisions such as moving to America has been relatively easy for me. If I feel strongly enough about doing something, I do it—regardless of what it takes. In that sense I have never been what they call "very sentimental." To be true to my higher path was always more important than attachment to places or things.

There were some furnishings and mementos, however, that I wanted to bring back to the States. These mementos represented my roots in Spain and I still have them in my home. Even though I am not usually sentimental, parting with some books and other things from school days, however, was painful for me. These I asked my husband to get rid of. "Don't even show them to me," I said.

Renting my house in Spain brought me a lot of problems that were not easy to solve at a distance, so I finally decided it was better to sell it. Selling the property was what I thought would cut all ties with Spain, but the Universe proved me wrong. After my mother's death, I reconnected with my cousins on my father's side of the family. My mother had never gotten along well with my father's family, and when I went to Spain to visit, she always told me not to call them. So, I followed her wishes since I was only there for a few days and did not want to argue with her. Now that I have established a relationship with these cousins, they are like brothers and sisters to me. I have found in them the family I never had. What's more, I could never have imagined that through them I would receive a baby—an event that would change my life forever.

5

BREAKING DOWN AND WAKING UP

My fiftieth birthday, two years after my mother's death, happened to coincide with the arrival of the new millennium. My birthday and my mother's death were significant milestones in my life and the year 2000 had always held a certain fascination for me. When I was a young girl and into my teenage years, I often wondered what my life would be like in the year 2000, where I would be in life and what I would be doing at age fifty. Mostly I wondered if I would live that long.

On the actual day of my birthday I fell into the biggest depression of my life. My husband had booked a nice spa hotel for the weekend and I can still see myself crying at ten o'clock at night while I was bathing in the swimming pool. My tears never stopped flowing for the entire weekend. I was inconsolable. I felt that my whole life had been a failure, that I had not accomplished anything and that I had wasted my life. I could see the look of helplessness on my husband's face. He felt powerless to help me. On and off through the years, I have had suicidal thoughts—and that day they surfaced powerfully.

Because I was so distraught, we decided to cut the weekend short and come back home early. We had just gotten our first pet three months earlier and, not only was I distraught, but it was the first time we had been separated from him.

I love animals and had always wanted to have a pet. I had set my mind on having a basset hound; I had no doubt that this was the dog for me. Perhaps from the bottom of my heart, I felt connected to this breed because their sad looking faces matched the feelings in my heart. *Feo, feo, feo.*

A friend of ours who was a dog trainer recommended that I become the foster mother of a basset hound before making the commitment of actually owning one. Since my husband was getting older and we were traveling less, he thought it might be the right time for me to get a pet. What I did not realize is that in my head I was asking for a basset hound, but, in my soul I was asking for a black cat. And of course, soul energy is what creates, not the mind, so it was no surprise that I ended up with a black cat. Years later, another black and white cat came to me, and one of my friends said, "These cats are your companions in the journey." In this instance, she meant my journey with cancer.

It was this black cat, Odin, we were going home to. Odin and Mittens too would turn out to be my most supportive friends during my experience with cancer.

Awakening

A friend of mine had schizophrenia and I took her for a psychic reading. The psychic advised her to learn to meditate and have psychic training at a school in San Francisco called Psychic Horizons. He told her this training would help with her health and teach her to control her symptoms. It would also help her have a happy life. She asked me if I would go to these classes with her, just to help her out. I agreed.

So we both went to a free introduction and made the commitment to start the classes together. Then the night before the first class, she called to let me know she was not going to the class the next day because someone had told her not to learn to meditate. I was really upset that she stood me up at the last minute but my husband advised me to go by myself anyway. He reminded me I had liked the introductory class and he said it would do me good to meditate.

At that time I was still going to the college and I felt I had enough classes already. The only reason I had signed up for the class was to help out this friend, but otherwise, there was no other reason for me to go. It was in this state of mind that I went to bed that night. It was the first time I had a dream that told me clearly what to do. This same type of dream experience has happened several times since. When my husband woke up the next day, he was surprised to see me already dressed and ready to go out the door. He said, "Didn't you say last night you were not going to the class?" I replied, "Yes, but I had a dream that I must go, so I am going to the class!" and I left.

That was the beginning of a major spiritual shift in my life. I attended six months of meditation classes and then I had to decide whether to continue with the psychic training or not. I had serious doubts about whether I could see and do readings because I had never been very self-confident. Although I remember telling myself, "Well, I am made of the same material as all these people and if they can see auras and do readings, why can't I?"

Also, I would need to spend many hours in the school and it

was a major time commitment. I was struggling with all these concerns when I had a second dream which dispelled any remaining doubts. By the end of the course I had gained enough confidence in my abilities that I did not need another dream to continue. Eventually, I became a teacher at the school. I spent eight years of my life in that school, four as a student and four as a teacher. This experience opened me up spiritually for all that would come later.

Illness and Intuition

Over the years I have had my share of health problems. One time I spent two years on and off crutches because of terrible pain in my ankle. The pain usually started after I had walked too much. It was so severe I could not even put my foot on the floor. When the doctor ordered an MRI to find out what was wrong, he told me the solution was so difficult it was better for me just to live with the problem.

One time the pain was so bad I passed out. My husband had to call 911 and they had to rush me to the hospital emergency room. This episode made me and my husband decide that I could not possibly continue like this. Something had to be done.

Three different doctors I visited reviewed the MRI and came to the same conclusion. They said I had a tumor in my Achilles tendon and needed surgery to remove it. They also advised that the surgery would cause damage to the tendon. They said I would need to be on crutches for a few weeks and wear a special boot for a few months after the procedure. Then I would need a second surgery to reconstruct the tendon. Further, there was no guarantee of a good result.

At this point, I was so tired of suffering with this condition that we decided to go ahead with the surgery. Because it was done under local anesthesia, I heard the doctor say, "Oh my God!" to which I immediately asked, "What do you mean by that?" To my surprise, he told me they all had interpreted the MRI incorrectly, and I actually had a tumor on my ankle, the type of which he had only seen on the knee. Apparently, this kind of tumor only grows on knees, not ankles, and they fully expected a quick recovery after it was removed. The surgery went smoothly and I was only on crutches for a week.

A few years after my ankle surgery, I started to have gallbladder attacks fairly often, but not bad enough to be taken to the hospital. I just endured the pain, however, I felt progressively worse until I could only eat oatmeal and white rice. I went to the doctor with these complaints. He prescribed some pills I never even took because I felt this medication was not the solution to my problem. Finally, one night I had another gallbladder attack and my husband took me to the doctor the next morning and told him we were not leaving until he diagnosed what was wrong with me. Well, we waited for the blood test results, and they promptly admitted me to the hospital because I had pancreatitis.

Since I had never been properly diagnosed and treated, the stones had blocked the ducts and produced the pancreatitis. They said I needed gallbladder surgery but I had to wait until the pancreatitis cleared up. They also found I had a mass in my liver, so there I was in the hospital for a week waiting for the pancreatitis to clear up so they could see whether I had liver cancer. Thank God all I had was a hemangioma, a blood tumor, but they also found a cyst in my kidney and a tumor on my adrenals. We still do not know whether this was the cause of my adrenals malfunctioning or if it was a result of the high stress in my life that produced such high levels of cortisol that my adrenals just stopped functioning normally.

They removed my gallbladder and it took me a long time to recover from the surgery. Since I have a hole in my heart, they gave me so many antibiotics to prevent a blood infection that I ended up with fungal infections and conjunctivitis constantly for the next six months.

To my surprise, I never vomited again after my gallbladder surgery. Until then, I thought vomiting was something that normally happens frequently, because as a child it was a real constant in my life.

Then, unbelievably, I fell on my back and suffered from a compression fracture. I was in such pain that I could not sit for three months. I could only stand or lie down. Fortunately, however, I recovered completely. I have had lower back pain on and off over the years, and later when I learned about Recall Healing, having lower back pain made total sense to me. I learned lower back pain is related to lack of support. I did not feel supported by my mother when I was growing up and eventually I did not feel supported by my husband in my married life. The feeling of not being supported became more and more constant.

Due to the poor health I was still experiencing even after my gallbladder surgery, my husband insisted I make an appointment to see his doctors at the Preventive Medical Clinic. The doctor ordered a series of tests. These tests showed that my body does not produce serotonin or lithium and therefore it was normal that I was depressed and did not feel much better with antidepressants. The doctor put me on a precursor of serotonin and lithium and my depression started to lift. I began to have a better outlook on life. After taking these supplements for only a short period, my health started to improve. At least I began to feel that life was bearable and more manageable than before.

Interestingly, during this time I was also diagnosed with Sjögren Syndrome (dry eyes and dry mouth due to malfunctioning of the parotid glands). This means I have the immune disease with the potential to develop into lupus and/or rheumatoid arthritis. However, for the first time in my life I decided not to be dominated by a diagnosis. I decided not to give this diagnosis—maybe any diagnosis—any power. In that moment I made the decision of not being afraid and I put the diagnosis out of my mind. Even though the numbers were coming back elevated, I was learning to trust my intuition. I refined my diet leaving gluten out of it. The beneficial results began to show up in the blood tests.

THE CRISIS DEEPENS

The Ship

My husband had infinite patience and I was able to experience this quality in him during the biggest crisis of our marriage. The biggest crisis of our marriage involved a ship.

A few years before we married, he bought a 150 foot triple deck ship that was moored in the San Francisco Bay. It was in inoperable condition because many years before it had been remodeled as a restaurant. This was a historical ship which was initially launched in 1922 from North Carolina. She sailed her maiden voyage through the Panama Canal to San Francisco.

The ship was originally built for the U.S. Army as a personnel carrier (ferry boat) and was used for that purpose in the San Francisco Bay and its tributaries during World War II. The ship is also listed in the U.S. National Registry of Historic Vessels. It was decommissioned in 1946 and sold for private use to a Mr. Crowley, who owned the largest tugboat business in San Francisco Bay. He subsequently sold the ship to Grey Line Tours who operated the boat for Bay Cruises between Alcatraz and San Francisco until 1955 when the ship was sold at auction.

The new owners moved the boat to Stockton where they took out the machinery and converted it to a floating restaurant which was subsequently moved to Jack London Square in Oakland. Later, it was moved to its present location, then known as the Sanchez Canal in Burlingame. My husband bought the ship in 1978 from the Keyston Brothers who represented the Anza Corporation which had a lease with the State of California.

My husband loved the water. He thought it would be ideal to have his office on the upper deck while leasing the restaurant downstairs to a third party. That is exactly what he did. Well, this ship turned out to be the only problem of our marriage. However the problem was massive. It caused the greatest stress between us and turned out to be one of the major causes of my cancer.

Just as we moved into the new house we had built for ourselves, we received a phone call at six o'clock in the morning telling us that the ship was sinking. It was moored in a canal that was not very deep, so it could not sink completely, but the water level had reached the top floor of the restaurant. The restaurant tenants had left a porthole open on a stormy night in January and that was enough to sink the ship. Water poured in through the porthole.

Thanks to my husband's children and a few friends, the ship was rescued in a few hours before it became a total loss. Bob's son dove into the water and closed the porthole, then, with many pumps all the water was pumped out. Nevertheless, all our savings went to repair the ship's damage. The project to decorate my house would have to wait. The ship began to rob me of what I thought was mine, and this pattern would continue. This ship saga turned out to be a constant strain on our marriage.

Ultimately, we decided the ship was more of a problem than it was worth. First, we decided to move my husband's office to our home. He would be retiring soon, anyway. Then, we decided to sell the ship. We did find a buyer. We disclosed all the details and history of the property, including the fact that a crime had taken place there. At one time, my husband had leased the ship to two partners, and one killed the other on the premises, mafia style, with one shot to each arm and leg and another shot to the heart. The new buyers were unfazed. They had big plans for the ship. They went ahead with the acquisition. It should be noted here that a ship is not considered real estate, rather it is private property and, therefore, there are no banks willing to loan money for this type of property. We would be required to carry the loan ourselves which is what we did.

Shortly after the sale, the buyers started having problems and were never able to carry out their plans. During all this time, my husband demonstrated remarkable patience by trying to help them find a third party to buy the ship and to see if they could find a way to fulfill their obligations in the contract with us. In the meantime, the ship was empty and was being vandalized. Bob was able to find a watchman to live there, although a lot of damage had already been done.

After ten years of doing nothing, the buyers walked away without meeting the terms of the contract. Finally, in 2001, we had to repossess the ship. The mooring lease with the State of California reverted to us too. We had two choices: to dismantle the ship or to restore it to resale condition. We were faced with a very big expense either way, and my husband was really attached to that boat. If we dismantled it, we would incur a major expense with nothing to gain. If we refurbished it and sold it again, we might come out ahead, so he opted for refurbishing it.

By then the ship had become a curse on our marriage. It was the only thing we argued about. Gradually she became the shadow we knew was there but always avoided. The ship really became "the other woman in my marriage." She took all an "other woman" might take.

I knew Bob was working with friends to restore the ship. I wondered where the money was coming from to do all the work. Every time I approached the money question, which was not very often, he would give me a vague answer. As always, neither of us wanted to argue, so we changed the subject and never addressed the issue.

Things were so tense I never went to the ship during those years. I did not want to hear anything about the place, even though it was where my husband went to work every day. Handling this problem had started taking up so much of his time and energy, there was not very much of him left for me or the marriage. I started to resent it.

Marriage Falling Apart

Years passed by like this until, in the spring of 2005, my husband announced that the work on the ship was almost finished. He said it was now in good enough condition to be sold. He was going to meet with the people who had helped him out with the project and wanted me to attend the meeting with him. I went to that meeting not knowing what to expect, but I certainly could never have anticipated what actually happened.

First of all, when I saw the ship after all those years, I realized that it was in much better shape than when we took it back, but certainly not in good enough condition to entice anyone to buy it.

Nevertheless, this deception was nothing compared to what was going to happen when the meeting started. I found out that my husband had borrowed half-a-million dollars from the people who had done the work on the ship, from members of his family, and from some friends. I learned about this massive debt in front of all these people. I managed to get through the meeting, but as soon as it was over and people started socializing, I could not contain my feelings any longer. I started crying and had to leave.

I think that was the saddest day of my life—even sadder than when I was diagnosed with cancer. When my husband arrived home that evening, he found me drowning in tears and enraged. How is it possible that he did not tell me about the debt before and waited to break the news to me in public? I remember my husband started crying too and told me he never expected that this situation would cause me so much pain. That very same day I moved out of our bedroom.

I realized later that it was during that meeting on the ship that the seed of my cancer was activated. It turns out, too, that where that seed was planted in my body was related to the ship. The seed was planted in my breast.

I was so sad and so full of anger that I could no longer talk to my husband. I blamed him for the situation I was in. I wanted out; that was all. We started going to counseling, as often as two or three days a week, because we just could not talk to each other without the counselor present. It was at that time I sought the advice of a divorce attorney to see if there was a way out of the debt and the marriage.

I had never stopped loving my husband, but I was really angry about the situation he had put me in. I blamed him entirely. (At that time I could not see the part I played by ignoring the situation for so long). When we talked about divorce, however, I still could not imagine living apart from him. I could not imagine not taking care of him, which by then had become such an integral part of my life. (You will remember he was thirty-four years older than me.) I wanted to find an arrangement by which, in spite of the divorce, we could continue together somehow.

This high stress situation lasted almost three months. Then, I remember one day waking up in the morning with a very clear head. I went down for breakfast and declared to my husband, "Until now, I thought that you were the one who put me in this situation and I was really angry at you and I only wanted to get out of it, but that is not true. God used you to put me here because I need to learn something from it. And I am willing to do so. Today I am going back to our bedroom. I am not going to divorce you and I am going to accept the problem we are facing the best way I can. I am going to start going to the ship on a regular basis. I will go three days a week, and I am going to bring the bookkeeping up to date. I am going to be in charge of all the money. You are only going to be in charge of the workers. We are going to try to find a solution to this. We'll do the best we can with the mess we're in." I remember my husband's face at that instant: a miracle was taking place in front of him. The miracle was that I changed my mind. I accepted the situation. I was returning to our bedroom. He gazed at me as if I were an angel.

Earlier the tension between us about the ship had always prevented us from finding a solution to the problem. Now, we created an LLC, something that should have been done years earlier, so we could protect our assets. I remember posting a classified ad in Penny Saver magazine to find someone to take the bar stools and chairs away for free. I wanted to take pictures of the ship and create a web site to start marketing it, something I had to do on my own. I contacted many real estate brokers but, of course, none of them wanted to take a listing for a ship that seemed to be almost impossible to sell, so we knew we were on our own to make something happen. An Irish man had taken the bar stools, and I urged my husband to contact him again to come back and take the chairs as he had committed to do. I was in a hurry to take the pictures for the web site and start a marketing campaign.

Then my husband told me that he had talked to the Irish man already and he was interested in buying the ship. My husband had asked for one-million-two-hundred-thousand dollars, and the Irish man had already agreed to the price. My husband told him he wanted half of the money as a down payment and then we would carry the mortgage for the balance owed. This was such an astonishing turn of events. Now it was me who was witnessing a miracle. My husband had always been positive. He trusted that we would find a buyer and get out of debt. And sure enough, he proved to be right. This all started in August of 2005 but it took until the spring of the following year to sign the contract. With the down payment, we were able to pay off all our debt and go back to "normal" life, although life never went back to normal again.

At that time, I was teaching part-time at Psychic Horizons. The meditations and classes helped me to get through our ordeal with the ship. Also, my husband proved to me how patience and optimism help to resolve problems. He never doubted that we would come out of it whole, and he was right. He always allowed me to move in the direction I wanted, because he wisely knew there are some things we cannot teach someone; we have to learn by ourselves when we are ready. As they say, "When the student is ready, the teacher will appear." Sometimes, the "teacher" is a series of events we have to deal with.

I should mention that I had quite a few readings at the psychic school about the ship. To my surprise, I was told that my husband was not the one who was attached to the ship, but rather that the ship was attached to my husband. He had been the only constant in her existence and the only one who had taken care of her properly on a regular basis.

My husband became very close to the new owner, helping him all he could by giving him advice and lending his expertise in dealing with the ship. Also, much of the assistance he provided was mainly negotiating with the city and state agencies to make sure the ship could reopen as a restaurant again. So, from all appearances, it seemed like my husband had a full time job again, and, at the end of the day, I only got a tired and worn-out man.

So once again, the "other woman" in my marriage loomed large. Since we had sold the ship, I rarely went there anymore. But I did go to the ship one day, and as soon as I parked the car in front of it, I saw that the old name of the ship, General Frank M. Coxe, had been replaced with a new name: The Sherman. That was his name, Bob's name. That was *our* name That was *my* name. I remember telling my husband at that very moment, "The 'other woman' in a marriage takes everything but never takes the man's name. In this case, she even took our name." Under the name of The Sherman the restaurant opened for business.

There were many celebrations and opening parties. My husband and I felt very differently about these occasions; I never attended any of them. Our marriage was so damaged after the crisis in the spring of 2005 that it never went back to the way it was. We continued going to counseling on and off for the rest of our time together.

TRANSITION

My Husband's Death

In April 2007, my husband's last sister passed away. On our way home after the memorial service and celebration of her life, I remember Bob saying, "It's a pity that we have these celebrations after people die. We should have them while they are still alive so we can tell them all the good things we feel about them instead of talking about them after it's too late, when they are gone." I told him, "Don't worry, you are going to have yours before you die, because as soon as that ship is finished and open for business, we are going to have a big party for all our friends and family to celebrate that your dream came true." I never knew that these words would end up having a literal meaning exactly a year later.

Although the restaurant opened for business on Christmas 2007, I decided to wait until the spring to have the celebration which would give me more time to prepare for it. Since many of my husband's friends were around his age, I thought it would be better to have the party when the days are longer and the weather is better. That is why I organized the party for April 5, 2008 to celebrate my husband's dream coming true: to have the ship restored and open for business in a situation we thought was "out of our hands." We had one hundred and fifty guests. That was the first day I went to the ship after it was opened. The celebration was at lunch time. We did not have too much time to eat because we were so busy taking care of the guests. Therefore, Bob and I stayed after the party was over to have dinner by ourselves. I could not have known that, after all we had gone through with the ship, it was going to be the first and last dinner we would have together there.

The day after the party, Bob spent the day resting and I spent it sending thank you cards. By the next morning Bob woke up with congestive heart failure. I rushed him to the emergency room. After a few hours, he had recovered but they decided to keep him in the hospital to perform an angiogram. I did tell the doctor that I did not think it was a good idea to do this test, because he had had one done several years earlier and did not react very well afterwards. Since he was older and weaker now, they left him in the hospital for observation.

Contrary to my request, the angiogram was scheduled when I was not there. I got really upset and left a note for the doctor to see me as soon as he arrived at the hospital the next day. When l arrived at the hospital early in the morning to talk to the doctor on the day the test was scheduled, it seems that as soon as he saw the note, he cancelled the procedure. Even so, it was too late: they had already given Bob Benadryl in preparation for the anesthesia to be administered for the test. He went to sleep and only woke up for a few moments after he was taken to the ICU, just long enough for us to hold hands and for me to tell him I loved him. He had an oxygen mask on and was only able to look at me in despair. The doctor told me he was dying. Then he went into a coma. I called his children. Then I spent all night talking to him and helping him to leave his body. He died the next morning on April 10' with his children and me by his side.

We all thought it was the ideal moment for his death, right after seeing the ship finished and having the celebration. In spite of the shock and the sadness, there was something to be happy about. His death, although sudden and unexpected, was not a complete surprise because he was ninety-two years old and, although well for his age, he was getting steadily weaker.

He always said that he wanted to be independent and drive until the end, and fortunately, his wish came true. His determination to continue driving made me worry, especially on days when he drove long distances. Although it made him happy to travel by himself, this had the opposite effect on me. It made me very nervous because I did not trust his ability anymore. This was a constant stress on my life.

When I married my husband, my father thought I was going to take care of an old man instead of him because of our thirty-four year age difference. Many other people assumed the same thing, but I must say that he was always independent, never bed-ridden and took care of himself every day of his life. I never had to do anything for him. We make so many assumptions that never turn out to be true! If we only would learn to be in present time and stop assuming a future that may never happen we would be so much better off.

Because I am an ordained minister—I was ordained when I graduated from Psychic Horizons—Bob had asked me to conduct his memorial service. I was afraid, though, that my voice was not going to hold up in public. So I wrote the memorial service with the help of a friend and asked him to conduct it for me. On the day before the service, I decided to have my own private ceremony for my husband. I wrote a letter to Bob, collected pictures, and played the song, "Because You Loved Me." This song really expressed my feelings at this moment very well. Yes, I began to understand I had become the woman I became because Bob Sherman had loved me. Bob Sherman loved me for being myself and his love gave me the freedom to blossom. He loved me in his own way, which was not always what I would have liked. I often demanded more from him than he was capable of giving. It took a long time for me to understand that he was doing the very best he could.

I spent time by myself privately reading the memorial I had written. This helped me to grieve the loss of my husband. Gradually, I began to come to peace with our relationship and the nature of our marriage.

After Bob's Death

At the time of Bob's death, my heart was giving me trouble. I was often tired and had shortness of breath. The doctors had scheduled some tests that I had to postpone because of the memorial and all the work that follows when someone dies. One month and ten days after his death, I lost consciousness and collapsed on the bathroom floor in the middle of the night. When I regained consciousness, I crawled into bed and did not feel very well when I woke up the next morning.

A friend insisted I make an appointment with the doctor to find out what was wrong. The doctor felt obligated to report my fainting incident to the Department of Motor Vehicles (DMV), but due to my being alone and not having anyone to drive me, he made the report in such a way that I did not lose my driver's license. It took me five months to resolve the issue with the DMV which included their requirement that I take the driving test again.

At this time, I had medical tests which showed that my heart was missing one-third of the beats that a normal heart has in a twenty-four hour period. The doctor remarked that these were a lot of beats to miss. He wanted to give me some medication, but I asked him to wait until some of my stress was relieved and things returned to normal before writing a prescription. I did not drink alcohol or caffeinated beverages, but I was under a lot of stress—and I had been for a long time. In a few months my heart did go back to normal. This heart episode would contribute to my decision as to how I would treat my cancer. This episode corroborated my feeling that my heart is the weakest part of my body. When I am under stress my heart is the most affected part of my body. My cancer would appear in the left breast and I certainly did not want radiation therapy anywhere near my heart.

By all appearances, everything seemed to be fine, including my accepting that Bob's life was over. I was grateful that he had lived such a long, productive life. However, I still had to deal with the fact that we had not received any payments on the mortgage we had agreed to carry on the sale of the ship. With the help of my accountant, I tried to get an agreement from the buyer to start the payments, but it was not long before he completely defaulted. To make matters worse, the restaurant was not doing well and on New Year's Eve 2009, he closed the restaurant and abandoned the ship.

I did not want the ship back, but there was still more than half-a-million dollars owed to me. So I hired a lawyer and planned to foreclose. I made the utility payments, looked for a real estate agent to find a buyer that the State of California would approve, and then I intended to sell the ship for whatever amount we could get. Also, I wanted cash, even if the amount was less. I just wanted this issue out of my life.

All seemed to go well. The real estate agent announced to me he had an offer, but, on the very same day, a man showed up in the ship's parking lot and told the realtor he was the ship's rightful owner. It turned out he was the man who had bought the ship at auction from the Grey Line Tour Company in 1955, twenty-three years before my husband bought it. This man had had the pink slip—something we did not know existed—since 1955. He had just re-registered the ship in his own name with the DMV and the Coast Guard. Of course this was after he found out the ship had been restored to a good condition, recently abandoned, and that my husband had died.

Understandably, this latest unforeseen development caused me an extreme level of anxiety. Now I would have to do a lot of research to resolve the ownership challenge. This was a costly process. (I would have enough material for another book on this part of my story, but today my subject matter is to tell you about my journey with cancer, what brought it to me and what brought me to it.) Finally, after some time fighting the battle of ownership, I realized that I did not have the money or the strength to continue. I did all I thought I could in my husband's memory and my own interest, but there came a time when I had to let go. I had to forgive everyone and move on with my own life so I would not die in this battle. I gave up the ship.

I had no idea at this time that another quite different battle was just around the bend.

6

AN UNEXPECTED JOURNEY

On February 7, 2011, the man who claimed to have been the owner all along changed the locks on the ship. It was a sign for me that the struggle was over. It would have been a sweet victory to win this ownership battle because of what the ship meant to my husband, but in another way, I was getting to the end of my strength and money and wanted to put this whole matter of the ship behind me. I wanted to move on, even if it meant losing what we had worked so hard to build.

I looked at the "time-life calendar" I created through the Recall Healing process and I saw that my uncle's death on February 7, when I was just seven years old, was the first loss of a beloved family member in my life. February 7 was also the day I made my first vows in the convent. Both of these events had come to be associated with a deep sense of loss for me. Another note: Bob and I got married twice. Our second wedding was on February 7. And now, on February 7, the man who claimed ownership to the ship changed the locks and took over.

With this turn of events, from that day forward, I decided to change my consciousness and try to focus on forgiveness.

By September, I was due for my annual mammogram. Afterwards, they told me to make another appointment for a second one and an ultrasound. When they finished the second mammogram, they decided to perform a biopsy instead of the ultrasound. One of my friends drove me to the clinic that day, and I remember telling her when I left the lab, "The surprise will be if I do not have cancer."

Two days later, the doctor called. I had cancer.

On that very night, I had a dream. My only clear recollection was the appearance of the number eleven. The dream clearly signified to me that something new was coming into my life, but I had no idea of what it meant and how my life would unfold. Since I had been diagnosed with cancer the previous day, death was in my mind. The dream made me wonder whether I was going to die.

My Reaction to the Diagnosis

It takes a while for a serious diagnosis like cancer to sink in, and although I told myself I had cancer, I did not want the idea of cancer to control me. I was determined to continue with my normal life, and so I was not prepared when cancer took over my entire life just one week later.

At that time, a friend from Spain, a cardiologist and a research fellow at Stanford Medical Center, offered to come with me to my doctor's appointments because she knew I had no family to support me. It was comforting and a relief that she would be with me to listen and take notes. She brought the added advantage of being a doctor herself.

We went to the surgeon together. The surgeon was very

efficient and explained that the surgery she recommended was a lumpectomy followed by radiation treatments. I had no problem with the idea of having another surgery, since I have had so many in my life already, so this concept was familiar to me. But the cancer was in the left breast, and I had a big problem having radiation therapy and putting my heart through this type of procedure; my heart which has carried me so long and so well despite the congenital abnormalities.

I have heard several times that the medical profession wants to create another branch of medicine called Oncocardiology due to all the problems that radiation therapy and chemotherapy cause to the heart. Knowing this, I expressed all my concerns to the surgeon about radiation therapy and asked her questions about the kind of cancer I had and where it was located exactly. In the back of my mind, though, what I really wanted to do was to go home and look in my Recall Healing books for more information about my type of cancer. I wanted to know everything about it. I found out a lot. As soon as I began to read these books everything became crystal clear to me.

The Cause of My Cancer

I had begun to study Recall Healing two years earlier. The way it started was simple. I am a member of a health and healing group that sponsored a series of three weekend workshops in Recall Healing with Dr. Gilbert Renaud. I attended the series, and because I found the concept of Recall Healing so intriguing, I had private consultations with him. I remember saying to Gilbert very early on "I have a big problem." My problem was the ship. I had already had the intuition, two years earlier, that the problem with the ship had the potential to make me ill. What I was learning about Recall Healing confirmed that idea. In fact, two years later, cancer appeared in my left breast. The day I was diagnosed, my first thought, concerning the cause, as I already mentioned, was The Ship.

In the theory of Recall Healing the first step towards healing is to identify the emotional trauma that caused the disease. If you do not recognize and heal the emotional cause of the disease, no matter how much physical treatment you undergo, you could possibly be "cured" but you will never be *healed*. If you don't address the underlying causes, the illness may return. This means we must look at illness in a different way. Not just cancer, but all illness.

To be cured is to have no more physical symptoms of the illness. You are cured when the tests come back clear and the doctors tell you they cannot find any trace of the illness in your body anymore. In the case of cancer, to be cured might imply not to die of the disease.

To be healed goes beyond that. To be healed is to have dealt with the cause of the illness at the emotional and even the spiritual level and to have healed whatever issue or issues brought you to have the illness in the first place. It is to have learned your lesson. It means you have reached a higher level of consciousness at the other end. This is why it is possible that you can be healed on your death bed.

Recall Healing is a method of self-healing consisting of the practices of "realizing it," "expressing it" and "releasing it."

"Realizing it" means discovering the cause. Sometimes we can become aware of the cause by ourselves although most of the time the cause of illness is stored in our subconscious mind and we need the help of someone else such as a therapist or a spiritual practitioner to discover it.

"Expressing it" means owning it. Sometimes this means making the cause publicly known, not necessarily in a book like I am doing, but to your family, to whomever is involved, or to the society you live in. Going public changes the energy pattern of the causal factors which helps healing happen on a broader level than just the personal.

"Releasing it" means letting it go out of your system. To do this people engage in practices such as healing ceremonies, writing letters to people involved in the cause, and practicing forgiveness. Each of us is different, and therefore, there is no formula that fits all. Each one, with the help of a teacher, must find his or her own way.

I had cancer in the left breast. In Recall Healing the left breast represents the mother if you are a right-handed woman. This was no surprise to me since I had had such an unhappy relationship with my mother. When I was a child, I never felt taken care of by her in the way I needed to be taken care of. Also, my biggest problem in the last years had been the ship. The relationship with my biological mother and the ship perfectly parallel each other. I believed having lobular cancer was connected to my feeling of being betrayed by my husband's business decisions with the ship, and I felt as abandoned by my husband as I had by my mother. Further, because I was no longer willing to nurture my husband and to continue "feeding him," metaphorically speaking, my breast milk had no outlet and was blocked. This was what my intuition was telling me. And, what is more, my mother, who was the protector of the house, is the one who indirectly was responsible for the sexual abuse I went through because the abuse took place in my own home. This also made sense. Really, I felt I had already healed, years earlier, everything related to my sexual abuse that was in my conscious mind, but I started wondering whether there was still something in my subconscious that I needed to reach and heal.

Then, when I looked at my ancestry according to the family relationships outlined in Recall Healing theory, things became even clearer. I was strongly related to two aunts, one on each side of my family, by birth order. These were the two aunts I would have most likely shared characteristics with, and as it turned out, they were the aunts I resonated with most all my life. One of them died of heart disease and the other of breast cancer—which are the two main illnesses that manifested within me. The aunt with breast cancer also had Sjögren Syndrome, so she had the same immune disease I have.

Next, I looked at my Recall Healing time-line which shows the repeating patterns during our lifetime. These patterns continue to repeat unless we become aware of them and act on them to change them. The way the time-line works is that our lives occur in specific cycles. These cycles consist of one's personal events that occur, for example, between conception and the first experience of independence. The patterns are different for each person, but the point is they repeat in regular intervals over the years. When I was diagnosed with cancer I was at the moment in my time-line cycle where I was reliving the pregnancy of my mother with me.

Finally, I looked at my "project purpose," another critical aspect of Recall Healing. The project purpose is what is implanted in the fetus or infant unconsciously by the parents during the time of conception, gestation, birth or the first year of life. The child will continue to live out this project purpose throughout his or her life unless he or she becomes aware of what it is. There was a strong chance that I would die at birth. This is the cellular memory my mother unconsciously implanted in me during the pregnancy. This made perfect sense when I revisited her pregnancy with me at the time I was diagnosed with cancer. According to Recall Healing, my project purpose was *death*. All my life I had been in a confrontation with death. Now, this confrontation became even more intensified.

Seeing the bigger picture and making these connections helped me understand the many factors that were the genesis of my cancer.

Also, I came to the conclusion that this tumor had actually been growing in me for three years. Two years earlier, in 2009, I went back for a second mammogram of the left breast because there was a slight irregularity in the first mammogram. I suspect that the cancer was already showing up, but probably was so tiny it was dismissed. The following year my mammogram was totally clear. I was in full fight mode with the ship conflict at this time. According to Recall Healing, cancer never shows up or grows in the middle of a fight; it grows when the battle is over. In 2011, the cancer started growing. This was the time I was working on trying to put the issue of the ship behind me and when I was trying to forgive the man who took the ship from me. When cancer showed up in the mammogram the process and progress of the cancer made perfect sense to me.

There are also many other causes of cancer that include genetics, pesticides, pollution, radiation and the carcinogenic environment we live in. I have no doubt that these conditions contribute to the immune system failing, but in my case, having the knowledge of Recall Healing allowed me to see many of the other reasons for my cancer.

Recall Healing was the beginning of my healing journey. I was determined to heal my cancer and I hoped that the cure would come with the healing.

7

MY HEALING JOURNEY BEGINS

I had to go for an MRI and then back to the surgeon who told me the cardiologist said that I could tolerate radiation therapy in spite of my heart problem. I just did not agree with the cardiologist's conclusion. He had only seen me twice and I had lived with my heart for sixty-one years. I felt I knew much more about my heart than he did. Since I did not agree to have radiation therapy, the surgeon then insisted I should have a mastectomy. It did not make sense to me to have a mastectomy for such a small tumor, and after thinking about this for a couple of days, I decided to cancel my surgery.

Next, I decided to consult with two other doctors: the one that was treating me already and was in the same office where my husband had gone for his alternative medicine treatments and another one who was referred by some friends. These consultations were a total disappointment. They told me that whatever cancer treatment I chose, they would support me but they offered no further suggestions. Afterwards, I found out that the problem was that I went to them with my friend who I introduced as a doctor. Both used alternative treatments that they were not ready to talk about in front of an allopathic doctor.

By then, I was completely distraught about not being able to find a treatment. My depression was even deeper when I walked out of the office after seeing these two doctors. I could sense that my friend was afraid for me because I was not following the conventional path. Even though my hopes were dashed when these two doctors offered me no support, I told my friend not to worry: I was not going to let myself die. I was going to treat the cancer but I just did not know how "yet." Not knowing what to do, I just cried and cried.

A friend of mine told me, "Your problem is that you are depressed when you should be angry," but I was never angry at the cancer. Cancer did not come from heaven, or better said, from hell. I knew exactly why I had it: my whole life had brought me to this point and this diagnosis. Everything fell into place perfectly, and how could I be angry about what I had unconsciously created? Everything happens for a reason and is for our good, even when it does not seem so at the time. It was important for me to learn my lessons and do my best with what I was learning.

My Friends' Reaction to Cancer

As my friends were learning about my diagnosis, the reaction I was getting back from all of them was "You? With your lifestyle?" They knew I was primarily a vegetarian and that I was very selective about my food choices. They considered my diet much better than theirs, so they were surprised about my cancer diagnosis.

With regard to exercise, I have never been very enthusiastic about it because I started exercising at thirty-two years of age after heart surgery, and I really never developed a fondness for it.

Nevertheless I still managed to go to the gym two days a week and to go to a dancing class. Yes, diet and the physical environment may have a lot to do with cancer, but none of my friends knew about my emotional state resulting from all the losses I had suffered, from mother to lamb to uncle to ship, not to mention my lifelong heart problem and the loss of a normal childhood, education and career due to the circumstances of my health and family.

From my friends' perspective, I always dressed fashionably, looked very well-groomed, could be counted on to meet social obligations and was always there for others. This was the way I presented myself to the outside world. My appearance was how I hid my lack of interest in life and the immense sadness I felt deep inside. Nevertheless, I think my friends' perceptions were right, and I have a hunch that the reason it took three years for the tumor to develop was because my lifestyle made it tougher for cancer to grow inside me.

Over the years, I had collected plenty of material for a cancer file on my computer, hoping I would never need it. Sometimes people just forwarded me information about cancer which I thought might be useful to someone at some point. I never imagined, however, I would be collecting this information for *me*. Now that it was the time when I needed to look at it, I was totally overwhelmed just opening the folder. My mind was confused not knowing where to start or how to do any investigation: it felt like climbing an impossible mountain.

I was alone with no family or close friends to help me out with the monumental task of facing cancer. I had many friends but now, having cancer, I realized they were not close friends and they were not going to help me in significant ways. That's when the sense of loneliness began to envelop me, a feeling that stayed with me all along my journey with this illness. Finally I decided to hire a Medical

Advocate to help me find a treatment and help me with my decisions. I had to pay for support that most people with family and friends have and take for granted. Needing to hire someone for this purpose is when I realized how alone I was in the world.

With the help of the Medical Advocate, I went back to the doctor at the preventive clinic where my husband had been treated. This time, without my doctor friend with me, the doctor suggested I consider going to Mexico for treatment by a doctor he works with who operates an inpatient clinic. But, after giving me all the information, he realized that he had not considered my history with depression. On second thought he said: "No, I cannot allow you to go there." The fact that I would have to go to Mexico alone, and live in a hotel room while receiving treatment, made him reconsider and conclude that it was not a wise idea for me to go by myself. I thought to myself, "I am too alone in the world to even treat my cancer."

By then, I had already started vitamin C IVs and was going to an acupuncturist regularly. I was so in need of her treatments that I had to go very often, and, in general, I was addressing my cancer physically with what I knew at the time while deciding how to move forward.

Note: "The" Breasts

I am becoming aware of the words I am using to describe cancer. I notice I use the phrase "my" cancer and "my" heart and "the" breast and "the" mother. I know how important language is and how we express ourselves can be so revealing. Now I am starting to consider the hidden meaning behind my word usage. It took me a while to realize that my language was expressing what my subconscious mind felt. I never felt connected to my breasts or to my mother, and therefore, I have been using "the" instead of "my."

To begin with I had very big breasts for most of my life, and I wore loose clothing to hide them as I was growing up. I really felt ashamed of my breasts. My breasts were a part of my body I always tried to avoid, so much so, that finally I decided to have breast reduction surgery.

The doctor was eager to perform a particular esthetic surgery that was so much in fashion at that time. I said: "No, I just want them smaller. That's all." I hated my breasts so much that it was out of the question for me to consider making them look better; I just wanted them smaller. I do not know how much of this had to do with my developing an illness in which one of the solutions is to take off the breasts. This might be something worth studying.

As it turned out, part of the treatment I would have to do for my cancer was light and sound therapy. This I am still doing as I am writing this book. The process of light and sound therapy requires applying light to my breasts and massaging them with a machine that emits certain sound vibrations. These are the therapies I like the least. I asked my doctor several times whether I could stop them, but he still insists that I should continue. And though I still feel disconnected with my breasts, I feel the day will come when I finally learn to love that part of me. There is no doubt in my mind that when I reach this point, it will coincide with the moment the doctor tells me to stop these therapies as they are no longer necessary.

I believe that everything has a meaning and the superficial events in our lives speak to us at a deeper level if we take the time to analyze and learn from them.

Note: "The" Mother

The closest I ever felt to being a mother was when I developed the deep relationship with my pet lamb during that summer at my mother's village. I was only six years old, but I was so traumatized with the way my lamb was taken away from me and his violent death that any feelings of motherhood in me closed down. It was too painful when they snatched "my" child from me, so it was safer not to have those kinds of feelings ever again. Really, this is how I have lived my life. I have avoided having dreams and desires so I would not suffer when they were taken away from me—as I knew they would be.

Most definitely, the conversation that the doctor had with my mother in my presence when I was nine years old, warning her that I should never have a child because I would die in childbirth, also remained in my subconscious mind.

These events, coupled with the unhappy relationship I had with my own mother, made me feel totally disconnected with the word "mother" and the notion of ever being a mother. Many years had to pass before my cats would help to bring the feelings of mothering back alive in me. And when my godson was born, which you will soon read about, I was finally able to experience a brand new life in my arms.

Dreams and My Decision to Go to the Clinic

Our Recall Healing teacher was coming to San Francisco to conduct a weekend seminar. I had already registered and paid for this seminar, and even though I did not think I would have the stamina to do very much that weekend, I decided to go anyway.

Typically the day would begin with a lecture analyzing whatever dreams from the night before the students presented to the teacher. And yes, I remembered very clearly the dream I had the night before the seminar. I recorded it in the dream diary I have been keeping for many years. In my dream, I was driving my car and was looking for a parking spot in a town square type area. When I put my car in reverse to park in a big space I had seen, there were two cars parked there already, so I continued in reverse to park the car in another place. When I finished parking the car, I realized I had parked it in a ditch. The walls of the ditch were as high as the car itself. Not knowing how I was going to get the car out of there, I started crying. Then a middle-age man with long white hair wearing jeans and a blue shirt appeared. He explained to me that he was the son of the owner of the post office which was just nearby. He handed me his card and told me not to worry at all because he was going to get me out of there.

When I related my dream to the class, I remember how happy people were to hear it. I myself did not know what to make of the dream. Although the message was comforting, it was clear to me that it was not realistic to wait for someone else to get me out of this situation. I knew I had to do the work myself.

The Recall Healing teacher, Dr. Gilbert Renaud, offered private consultations, and we started to work together on my healing. When I explained to him how lost I felt about the best way to proceed with my treatments, he told me he knew a doctor with a clinic in Mexico who had studied Recall Healing with him. I immediately asked for his name. I went to the internet and read all about his clinic. I asked for a phone consultation. He had the same beliefs about cancer as I did. We both studied with the same teacher and both of us believed that cancer was not only caused by genetics and external physical causes, but also that our mind, our emotions and the way we deal with life itself has a lot to do with it.

Just before I talked to him, I had another dream where I received the message: "Have the surgery and go to Mexico." So when we spoke, I asked him whether to have the surgery before or after going to his clinic for treatment. He replied that he thought it would be better to go to his clinic to have the treatment first, so that when I had the surgery later, hopefully the cancer would be dead and would not spread. In his experience, a couple of his patients had successfully followed this protocol.

When I asked him how much experience he had had with patients like me, I appreciated his honesty when he replied: "Not much. Normally most of my patients come to me not when they have just been diagnosed like you, but after they have had surgery, gone through radiation therapy and/or chemotherapy, and finally, when they have lost all hope with allopathic medicine. That's when they think about coming here."

My Medical Advocate was also present during this conversation with him, and after consulting with her, we liked the idea of my going there. He had an inpatient clinic, which is exactly what I needed because I was going alone, so it seemed everything was falling nicely into place. I went to my alternative medicine doctor here and told him I had found this clinic in Mexico, and since it was an inpatient clinic, it was the ideal place for me to go. I put the two doctors in communication with each other, because one would have to treat me in Mexico and the other would need to help me with the treatments when I came home.

The only choice I needed to make was when to go there. I very consciously decided to start the treatment on 11/11/11. On exactly that date, I had made reservations to go to Arizona with a friend to attend a David Wilcock seminar. David Wilcock is a spiritual teacher who I am fond of. It was important to me to be at his seminar on such an important date. Of course, I cancelled when I found out about my cancer. What I did not know at the time is that on that precise date, 11/11/11, I was about to start what would become "my own seminar," the most important seminar of my life.

I told everyone I was going to the clinic without a computer because I just wanted that time for myself and to concentrate on my own healing, which was true, but I still took my computer anyway to have the freedom of using it for my own interests and needs, but not to be in contact with anyone.

From the time I was diagnosed to the time of making the decision to get treatment at this clinic instead of going with allopathic medicine, I was under tremendous stress provoked by the arguments I had with some of my friends who were against my decision. What decision? Many believed I was turning my back on allopathic medicine, which they considered to be a superior system. I did not have anything against allopathic medicine or its treatment, I just believed it was not the appropriate path for me at that moment. I just had to follow my intuition. This was part of the reason I told everyone I would not have my computer with me. I knew my friends had the best of intentions with their opinions and advice, but they just could not understand what I was doing. I know that some of them even thought I was committing suicide because of not following the conventional way to treat cancer. I had to stand my ground, even with the risk of losing friendships, which for me, not having close family, meant a lot.

My Family's Reaction to My Cancer

My cousins in Spain are the only family I have, and I must say that to my surprise, they were always supportive of whatever decision I made. They were there for me all the way. It was nice to feel loved and respected, no matter what. I knew I had a family in them, but until I had cancer, we had not gone through a crisis where I needed their support. They stepped up to the plate to help me as any close family would do. In this case, stepping up to the plate meant not judging me. They listened to my whole story on email or by phone. They sympathized and supported me without ever giving me advice or their opinions.

These cousins turned out to be the grandparents and parents of my godson, the newborn baby who would play a major role in my healing process.

The Mexican Clinic

Arriving at the clinic forced me to face the fact that I "really" had cancer and that I needed treatment. It is not that I did not recognize what that diagnosis meant before, but now I had to look at it from another perspective.

It was a comfort that we all spoke Spanish—and the fact that I was there alone helped me to get close to others, especially the female nurses. We developed a great relationship very quickly, and I told them they were my Mexican family.

The hyperthermia treatment was one of the most difficult therapies for me because I was not used to the heat level, and although I am not claustrophobic, I felt really confined and uncomfortable during this treatment. They put me in a tube where it was impossible to move, and I only had the freedom to move my head. Sometimes, when it was too hot to tolerate, the nurses put a fan nearby. They would sit and talk to me for as long as they could as a way of distracting me from the discomfort.

Since I spoke Spanish one of the nurses gave me a book she

was reading: "*Yo (no) Quiero Tener Cancer*" (translated means "I Do (not) Want to Have Cancer") by Jennifer Middleton, a psychologist in Chile who had worked with cancer patients for twenty-five years. She discovered that all cancer patients have something in common with each other—either their emotions or their behavior and/or the way they handle life. In some ways her book corroborated what I already had learned from my Recall Healing studies. I noticed that only half of the book was underlined, so I guessed the nurse had not finished reading it when she gave it to me. The book was not too long, so I was able to finish it quickly and return it to her. She did not want it back and offered it to me to keep as a reference should I ever need it. Generous and thoughtful gestures like this happened almost daily from all who were working at the clinic. I felt so loved and nurtured by everyone who helped me during my stay even though some of the treatments were difficult to go through and made me feel sick.

Being at the clinic was to live "immersed in cancer" where all the doubts and questions about survival came to the surface. Although doing so many therapies occupied most of my time there, everything was a reminder of the cancer—and sometimes depression kicked in. As soon as the nurses noticed that I was depressed, they took turns being with me as much as possible. I will never forget their kindness and how cared for I felt by all of them. I think their efforts towards me were even more noticeable because I was there alone. Everyone else was there with one or more family members. I was one of the few patients there by myself—alone with my cancer.

The Dentist

In some cancer treatments, dental work becomes a very important issue. Having a dental checkup was part of my initial evaluation at the Mexican Clinic. I had two root canals which needed to be removed because root canals can be a source of chronic infection. When the immune system is functioning well, it can manage any low level infection. When the immune system is overburdened, even a low level infection in the root canal system could cause health issues such as cancer in the organ on the same acupuncture meridian. According to this acupuncture meridian system, when a tooth becomes infected or diseased, the organ on the same acupuncture meridian can also become unhealthy. As I found out later, the root canal in the top left tooth in my mouth was just one tooth off of the breast meridian, and the one on the lower right tooth was right on the breast meridian. This was another discovery about my cancer that made sense to me.

Note: "My" Cancer

I have often been asked why I call it "my" cancer. I have been told to stop saying it this way because "my" is not an appropriate adjective to use with the word cancer. In my experience, I knew too much about my cancer and its causes to look at it like an outside "problem" that had simply landed in my lap. I think I instinctively called it "my cancer" because it came from my soul. In the same way that I understood the process that had caused it, I was now trying to discover the process of how to heal myself with the hope of being cured one day. Cancer really was becoming my teacher, and the relationship I was developing with cancer was helping me discover more about myself.

I have never rejected any experience life has offered me, including everything from being sick in childhood, to having my young dreams broken, to leaving the convent, to having open heart surgery in a foreign country. Through all my illnesses, through all the problems in my marriage because of the ship, and now through my cancer, I had assimilated all these experiences and did not reject any of them. They have been lessons I have learned from. As one of my friends said, "You have not even rejected cancer."

The two weeks at the clinic went by very fast at the beginning and then very slowly toward the end. I so looked forward to being in my own home again—and it seemed to take forever for the return date to arrive. When it was finally time to leave, I came back with some good news: my tumor had shrunk during the time I was there.

8

LOST IN THE DESERT

What I did not realize when I went to the Mexican Clinic was how many of the therapies I would still have to do myself after I came home. The therapies occupied half of my day. Also, I came back with a port that I had to take care of. A port is a hole in your vein just under the clavicle that makes the veins accessible for an IV. When it is temporary like mine was, it requires certain care so it does not get infected, and I knew that if it did get infected, the infection would go right into my blood stream. Because of the hole in my heart, I would have only a slight chance of overcoming it and I could easily die from an infection instead of from the cancer itself.

I felt very uneasy and insecure about some of the therapies I had to do. I remember waiting for my housekeeper to come on the first day that I had to give myself an IV. I felt some relief knowing that at least I was not home alone if anything should happen. Really, I was taking the process of healing into my own hands to the fullest extent and this contributed to the spiritual journey I would find myself embarking on.

My Loneliness Increases

About a week after I came back from the clinic, it was my birthday. It just happened that most of my closest friends, or those I considered to be my closest friends, forgot my birthday that year. This was the year I needed the most support from my friends—but I never got a phone call, a visit, or even a card. It was my impression that since I was not around as a reminder, I was very quickly forgotten on my own special day. Maybe this was a message from the Universe that actually served me by giving me a theme for my meditations: being so isolated had intensified the feeling of loneliness cancer had brought me, and going through this experience also made me realize that I really had been alone nearly all my life.

Due to my heart problem and being an only child, I had a very lonely childhood. During my teenage years and all my years living in Spain, I had a couple of close friends, but time and distance separated us. I was so accustomed to being alone, and solitude was so much a part of my identity, that I even chose to enter a cloistered convent where it was impossible to talk to anyone.

As a continuation of this pattern, I then married a very private man who rarely communicated about himself or his feelings. My marriage really had been more of a monologue than a dialogue. Over the years I had made friends as I am an open and sociable person by nature. But I came to realize that these friendships were not very deep, because, in times of trouble, when I really needed them the most, they were not there for me. Cancer made me realize that the loneliness I felt was nothing new. Loneliness had been a constant in my life and cancer shook me to my core. As part of the process of dealing with cancer, I began to evaluate the extent of my loneliness.

I remember talking to friends about this feeling and was

surprised at how offended they were and how defensive they became. Their typical position was that we are all alone. However, I was trying to convey something very different than the existential loneliness we all feel. Rather, I was trying to express the loneliness of not having family or a close friend around to communicate with on a regular basis. I felt misunderstood. I did not want to hurt my friends, who meant so much to me, so I just decided to keep my feelings to myself. This heightened my loneliness and inward focus even more.

My Depression Deepens

Christmas came and went, and in the middle of January, I felt deeply depressed. I hit rock bottom. My depression was far worse than it had been in many years, and finally I realized that, in the same way that I was spending money on my medical treatments, I had to do the same for my emotional needs. I chose to go back to the same therapist that my husband and I had gone to for marriage counseling. She was local, easy to reach, and she knew my background so I did not need to start from zero. Sometimes I did not have "major problems" to talk about or have a need to ask for her help to solve a problem, but I was sure I could not go through the cancer experience by myself any longer.

Just after I brought her up-to-date with what was going on in my life, one of the first things she told me was that I needed to make new friends. Sure enough, cancer and all the spiritual work I was doing were changing my vibration and some of my old friends did not fit any more. Over time, this awareness has become clearer to me.

All those months of reclusive living and doing intense therapies at home made me recognize that I had more discipline and patience than I could have ever imagined. As it turns out all the constrictions I experienced during my childhood due to my heart problem, my two years in the convent, and the circumstances in my marriage had taught me everything I needed to navigate this time in my life.

Also, I had been working with dreams for several years and now my dreams helped me even more. The guidance I received from dreams—such as whether I should start a new therapy—became invaluable. My intuition was becoming increasingly stronger. I began to realize I had some resources which might help me heal myself from cancer.

Further, I remember telling my husband many times that I did not want to die suddenly as I wanted to have the experience of knowing I was dying. I am sure there is a lot to learn during the passage of death, and I have always been eager for this knowledge. I do not want to miss this lesson. Well, here I was dealing with cancer and perhaps facing my own death. Certainly the Universe was honoring my request.

And, because of the way I chose to treat my cancer, I began to meet many people who were doing likewise. I started to make new and lasting friendships—because we had this experience of having cancer in common. If I had chosen surgery and radiation therapy instead of the treatments I chose, I would not have had the opportunity to develop these important relationships. When I learned that some of my new friends were dying, I gained a new perspective about life and death. I began to reevaluate what life means and how death goes unaddressed. We avoid thinking about death; we do not recognize it as a natural and normal part of life. But death is natural and normal and death can be a great teacher.

By February, I was due for more tests. My insurance company was willing to do an MRI even though they did not agree with the kind of treatment I was doing. When the results came back, it was obvious that my tumor had shrunk to about half the size it had been. So, my approach was effective. Also, in February, I had to go back to the clinic in Mexico to have the temporary port removed. While there, I had an ultrasound which confirmed that the tumor was half its previous size.

Without the port and with the tumor shrinking, I began to feel much more secure. I started dancing again. I went to a dancing class. What could have been more joyful!

Dr. Gilbert Renaud came back to San Francisco again to give us a healing seminar. I was intensely interested in each session; and I scheduled private consultations as well. We worked hard on my healing, clearing even more of my life issues to help me move on. Part of this was creating new projects, which was the biggest challenge for me. Physically I was doing all I had to do to heal according to the methods I had chosen, but still I was living without a purpose for the future. I knew my greatest challenge would be to break the pattern of thinking anything I desired would be taken away—just like the lamb of my childhood. Gilbert told me to make a list of the things I wanted to do in the next two years. It was such a struggle for me to come up with a list, but I was determined to do it. I remember the first item on my list: to deepen my relationships with people.

9

THE HEALING

One day when I was in my kitchen hooked to an IV, I had a sudden flash of memory about a Tarot reading three years earlier when my friend said, "Unless you dedicate your life to metaphysics you will get sick." There I was, attached to an IV and dealing with cancer!

I had a resurgence of energy after all the work I had done with Gilbert and I was ready to start coming out of my cave to re-engage in the world. I was ready to study metaphysics. I had been so isolated for almost a year. It was time to start living, even with cancer. I found out about a Tarot seminar which was taking place near my house, so I decided to check it out. Well, it just so happened that the Tarot teacher taught a Kabbalah class on the internet, and as she was ten minutes from my house, I would be able to have regular meetings with her in person. This became a turning point in my spiritual life. This was the metaphysical quest I was looking for.

Also at the same time, I found out about another Kabbalah class every Thursday evening which I started to attend. Everything was coming together. My life was starting to take shape. I listened to what my heart was longing for and seized the opportunities that came my way. I began to learn more about metaphysics. I began to attend to my spiritual life instead of constantly worrying about my therapies and my survival.

I had never written anything in my life except for entries into my dream diary. The dream state had always interested me more than life in the physical world. However, now that I had signed up for the Kabbalah class, I was required to keep a journal about my experience with the kabalistic *Tarot of the Spirit* cards we were studying in the course. With each card, there was a set of questions we were supposed to answer about whatever spiritual issues came up around that specific card. We were to record our answers in our journal. Many times the question had to do with our desires and our visions for the future. In the beginning, I could not find answers to those questions. I was not accustomed to thinking about physical life or the future. But all that was about to change.

Fashion Comes Alive

As part of the Kabbalah class we were instructed to find something creative to do. At first, I was totally lost about what to choose. Out of a suggestion from Pamela Eakins, the author of *Tarot of the Spirit*—my Kabbalah teacher—I realized I had been cutting out and saving pictures from a Spanish magazine I have subscribed to since moving to the United States. All the pictures were filed in several folders that I kept in a file cabinet. After the first prompt from Pamela, I decided to put them in albums so at least I could enjoy looking at them.

I had thought about doing this a few years ago, but I always dismissed the idea because I thought it was a waste of time. All my life I believed I would die, and as you will remember, when I studied Recall Healing, I discovered death was my "project purpose." My entire life journey had been organized around death and dying. Why would I want to paste pictures into a book?

I still had my doubts when I started this project, but then everything began to fall into place very naturally and—I started to get excited. When I went to buy the albums, they happened to be on sale at half-price. Even when I needed to buy more albums as the collection expanded, I always found them on sale. This seemed like a sign from the Universe; this was the project I was meant to do.

When I began cutting, clipping, and dividing the pictures into categories and gluing them in the albums, I experienced a new sense of well-being and happiness that I had not known in a very long time. As a little girl, I spent a lot of my time by myself collecting, cutting and dressing paper dolls because I could not go out and play. I remember going every week without fail to buy the new booklet with the latest new doll and dress collection. This was something I always looked forward to; it was the highlight of my week as a child. These same feelings of delight, ones I had not known since I was a little girl, were coming back to me.

Although I made a great effort to create these albums, it is now a breeze for me to add new pictures to keep the collection up-to-date. It is so much fun and has become an enjoyable hobby. This was the first life-affirming project I did after my diagnosis and it was an ideal distraction from the cancer. As I cut and pasted, I was able, for the first time, to forget entirely about my illness.

Around this time a friend of mine, Donna Scheifler, began to teach Your Time to Blossom. It was a class for women over fifty: women in a life transition. One of the assignments for the class was to make a collage. Since my friend knew I was putting together these albums about fashion, she recommended that my fashion albums should be the "collage" project I should work with. As I was making the album with wedding dresses, I was inspired to write questions about the feelings those dresses evoked in me. I also created the answers. These were some of the questions that became captions for the gowns:

"What are you marrying?"

"Does it need to be a conventional wedding?"

"What are you looking for?"

"Have you embroidered your wedding dress?"

"Do you care about what other people say?"

"Who helped you prepare for this wedding?"

"Do pearls represent tears in the marriage?"

"Go ahead with your resolution! What about stepping out of the box?"

"What are you in love with?"

"Who are you sharing the cake with?"

"Does age matter?"

"What are you longing for?"

"Are you ready to dance?"

The answers read like this:

"Be different! Be yourself!"

All these questions and answers were accompanied by many glamorous pictures of elegant, and in many cases, quite unconventional wedding dresses. These became my meditation themes. I began to get in touch with a part of myself that I knew existed but had never been exposed so overtly. I finally realized that what I was searching for was my own soul and the marriage to myself.

Oh, my, I was beginning to fall in love again.

Going to the Movies

It was Oscar season. Every year around this time I would get excited about seeing the movies that were nominated for Academy Awards. I remember going with a friend to see *The Life of Pi*. When the movie was over, my friend commented about my obvious discomfort and tears during the movie. To me, the movie was like looking at my own life—alone in the vast ocean with a tiger keeping me alive. At the same time, the tiger was what could kill me. This was the perfect allegory for my situation with cancer. Even the evolution of the character's relationship with the tiger was the same evolution as my relationship with my own cancer. This story was a reflection of the ordeal I was experiencing. The same surprise I got when I found out I had cancer was the surprise the character experienced when he found the tiger on the boat. He realized that he and the tiger had to live together. He would have to provide food for the tiger if he did not want to be devoured by him—just like I had to do with cancer therapies. I had to acknowledge my cancer to not be killed by it. Caring for the tiger gave the character a sense of purpose and the motivation to continue fighting to stay alive in the middle of the ocean. I was fighting to stay alive too—alone with my cancer. We both, the character and I, had found a similar purpose in life. As time goes by in the movie and the battle is so long, both characters start getting weaker. As they weaken, their relationship begins to deepen to the point that the character is finally able to caress the tiger. The same thing happened with me. As time passed, cancer became less of a stranger to me. I started thinking of him as my teacher. In *The Life of Pi* the characters were bound together until the lesson was learned and the spirit was free. By then, incredibly, the character had come to love the tiger. Why? Because the tiger was what kept him alive. In the end, it became painful when the tiger ran off into the forest without saying goodbye, but the hero was now freed. He didn't need the tiger anymore.

Two weeks later I went with the same friend to see an Australian movie called *The Burning Man*. We had only read one article about the storyline, and in the storyline, cancer was never mentioned at all. Well, while watching the movie, we were surprised to discover that half of the movie was about breast cancer. It was about how this young couple deals with breast cancer—until the woman dies. As soon as we walked out of the movie theater, my friend apologized for going to see a movie about cancer. But, while I was watching the movie, I did not see myself at all in the story. I felt more like a spectator. How the main characters were dealing with their cancer was much different than the way I had chosen to deal with mine, and so the subject did not affect me emotionally. However, when it came to *The Life of Pi,* I totally identified with the main character. *The Life of Pi* was my story.

Back to Metaphysics

I had been studying Kabbalah from the courses Pamela Eakins was teaching based on her books, *The Lightening Papers, Ten Powers of Evolution* and *Tarot of the Spirit.* Studying with her for a few months is what really put me on the path to spiritual healing. Many times, while reading the weekly assignments, I would start to cry and could not stop. I was getting in touch with feelings that had been suppressed for such a long time, and I was overwhelmed by the realizations that came to me while reading the material and doing the meditations. I would often just burst into tears. In the beginning, finding the answers to the questions in the weekly lessons was extremely difficult for me. It forced me to face how shut off I was to life and how lost I felt. I had never allowed myself to dream of a future—and many of the questions were future-oriented. But, as I became more engaged with the project purpose of *living*, finding answers became easier and easier.

Everything was starting to come together. While reading Pamela's *The Lightning Papers*—where the chapters correspond to the spheres of the Kabbalah—I had a sudden revelation. I was on Chapter Six, all about the sixth sphere of the Kabbalah. The sixth sphere is called the spiritual heart of the Kabbalah. Suddenly, I got in touch with the spiritual connection that had developed out of the relationship I had established with my physical heart over the years. This revelation was the beginning of what brought me back to Life. Finding that first deep personal answer about the relationship of my own heart to the heart of the Cosmos was like finding the birth of a river and never being able to stop the stream again: life had started to flow.

Synchronicities started happening every week. My daily life started aligning with the pattern in the Kabbalah which was the same as the pattern in the *Tarot of the Spirit* cards. I began to anticipate the next card and the next lesson, and I just could not avoid growing with it at a pace and rhythm I had never expected. Kabbalah is the Tree of Life, and certainly I had started to climb it. Now nothing could stop me. I knew that if I had to die, I was going to die healed and that I would become *alive* in the process. Now I had found the tools.

I was studying metaphysics—and I was going to get well.

Meeting the Oncologist

It was February again, and my insurance company kept insisting that I had to have surgery. They ordered an MRI. The good news was that the tumor had not changed, but my lymph nodes were still swollen. They were concerned that the cancer might have spread to them. I insisted on getting a referral to an oncologist because I had been diagnosed with cancer for more than a year, and I had not yet seen an oncologist. That is because I had not followed the prescribed route for treatment.

When I met with the oncologist and answered the usual questions, the questions I had been asked every time I went to see a new doctor, I had to explain that I had no family—which is the reason I was there alone. The oncologist told me he was afraid of cancer, and it seemed as though he wanted to instill fear in me so I would follow the more accepted route of having a lumpectomy followed by radiation therapy or a mastectomy. According to my insurance provider, I had not treated my cancer *at all* and the only way they knew how to convince me to have surgery was to scare me into it. I recall making some remarks to him that he should not be inflicting such fear on his patients. But he proceeded to explain to me how much more my tumor was going to grow, how bad it was going to smell, and that I was going to die if I did not have the surgery. (It crossed my mind in that moment that the Tarot reader said I would get sick if I didn't study metaphysics.) I was already fearful about having cancer and did not appreciate his comments. It is hard enough to live in this world as it is without being influenced by the negativity that has been created around this illness. By this time, I had started to learn to live with my cancer; I was only just beginning to overcome my fear. Instead of cancer being my enemy, it was quietly emerging as my teacher.

When I left the oncologist's office, I called a friend and told her the whole story about what he told me. I finished by saying, "He was a nice man." My friend confessed to me the next day that she was completely baffled that I made that remark after hearing everything he had said to me. By this time I had learned a lot about the allopathic perspective on cancer and understood that there were many alternative points of view. My purpose in meeting with the oncologist was to listen and get information, not to convince anyone about my position. I wanted his information; I also wanted to make my own decisions according to my own belief system and intuition. The oncologist commented that I was unique in that they had never had a patient like me: someone who rejected conventional treatment and decided to deal with cancer in her own way. He understood I wanted a special surgeon and agreed to help me find the right one for me. I told him I had to think about it and would get back to him when I was ready.

A Baby on the Way and Death in the Mix

While I was in the middle of the cancer treatment, during one of my darkest moments, I received a call from Spain. It was the daughter of my cousin who wanted to let me know she was pregnant. She had come to visit me twice, one time with her sister and the other time with her husband. We had become very close and always enjoyed each other's company. She had been married for six years and finally decided to have a child. It was such good news. I was very, very happy for her.

It never occurred to me that this event was going to mean so much to me—and my recovery.

My cousin subscribed to a service through the internet that shows the baby's growth in the womb every week. She shared this with me so I could follow her whole pregnancy. All my life I had been totally removed from pregnancies and births, and now when I was dealing with cancer and may be facing my own death, here I was following a pregnancy—extremely closely—and expecting a new life.

I was still physically and emotionally tired. One-and-a-half years after my diagnosis, I was still giving myself therapeutic treatments at home and going to the doctor for weekly treatments, all the while wondering whether my cancer was in remission or if it had spread. I was still torn about whether to have surgery or not.

By this time, I had done a lot of healing physically, emotionally and spiritually, and I was hoping that my tumor might now have very little activity and would almost be dead. I had approached my illness like a spiritual journey, and I wanted to do the best for my spiritual growth. Of course, I wanted to live as well. At last, I was starting to feel how it feels to be alive and my interest in living was becoming stronger.

I started to become extremely excited about this new baby coming into the world. Here was new hope! Here was profound relationship! Here was *family!*

When I was having these insights, when I was studying Kabbalah and meditating with the cards, sometimes I had insights where I recognized that not having family and being alone in the world was an asset in one way because there was no one to push me in one direction or another. I was free to choose what direction I wanted to go with my illness. But, at the same time, it was difficult to make decisions alone. With the new baby on the way, I began to feel I was not alone—maybe.

With the baby coming I kept thinking about birth and death,

change and changelessness. What is being born? What is eternal? What never changes? One thing is for certain: I knew a new baby was on its way in.

One day I said to my therapist, "My goal is to come to a point when the outcome of my illness does not matter to me, whether I live or die would be meaningless." I had been listening to an audiotape of Wayne Dyer's book, *Wishes Fulfilled*, and the phrase, "I am birthless and deathless and changeless" really stayed with me. I remember my therapist answering, "Don't be surprised if you never arrive at that goal. While we are in a body, we are attached to it." As I thought about it more, what I meant was that I wanted to die "healed" regardless of whether or not I was cancer-free ("cured"). I wanted to be whole in spirit, heart and mind—with all the causes of my cancer identified, understood and addressed. Hopefully, then my body would heal as well.

Throughout all my life I have had an ideal of death. For me, a person who is healed can let go of life easily and freely and beautifully. I remember a story I heard about Joachim and Anna, the parents of the Virgin Mary. The storyteller said that when Joachim's time came to die he told Anna, simply, "It is my time to leave the body. I will be leaving it soon—during meditation." Anna served him and witnessed him during his passing. In meditation, then, he left his body—consciously and gently—without illness or pain. To me, this is the ideal way to die.

And—healing would be the ideal kind of birth.

I was having the profound insight that achieving that detachment from the physical outcome of my illness was the new healing quest I was on.

Meeting John of God

Around this time, I received an email from a friend telling me that John of God, said to be a great healer, was going to be in Toronto in two weeks. She wanted to know if I would join her there. Certainly Toronto was closer than Brazil, where he resides. It did not take me long to make the arrangements for the trip. The idea of seeing John of God was not totally new to me since I had known about him long before my diagnosis. I had considered going to see him years before. Well, now the opportunity came my way.

During this illness I have said *yes* to many things that were presented to me for healing—and John of God was one more.

John of God is considered to be one of the most powerful healers in the world today. His healing center is in Abadiania, Brazil. He is reputed to be a medium whose body is used by many spiritual entities to perform miraculous healing. The entities include saints such as St. Ignatius of Loyola, the founder of the Jesuits, the Biblical King Solomon, and deceased doctors such as Dr. Oswaldo Cruz who eradicated yellow fever in Brazil. As a full-trance medium, John of God has no recollection of the work performed through him during the healing sessions. He always says, "I do not heal anyone. The only one who heals is God."

Definitely I wanted physical healing, but if I could not achieve this result, at least I wanted to come back with a peace of mind I did not have before going on this trip. I was not getting information in my dreams about whether I should have surgery or not, so when I left to see John of God I was in a tense state of mind. I was hoping that after seeing him, I would return home at peace with myself and I would be able to make a clear decision about having surgery.

During the flight to Toronto, I went through one of the

worst experiences of terror that I have ever had in my life. I felt overwhelmed by fear and paranoid thoughts of being kidnapped and killed on my arrival. I feared it would take days for anyone to discover my fate, since I do not have any family or close contacts who would think to look for me. The fact that I would think such negative thoughts shocked me, because I travel to Spain alone frequently and had been to several countries by myself even before I got married. It seemed impossible that I was suddenly experiencing this kind of fear.

This incident made me realize I had been "in my cave" for too long. This was the first time I was going somewhere other than to the clinic in Mexico. Suddenly, I remembered what my therapist had explained to me about these feelings of insecurity that cancer brings, and I started doing the exercises she taught me to do. I began to practice disengaging from my thoughts by remembering that my thoughts were not me. Thoughts are not real; they are products of the imagination. By the time the plane landed in Toronto I was happy, secure within myself, and ready to be healed.

There were thousands of people attending the event. I think there were more people than they were really prepared for, so the organization of the event was not quite as I had expected. During the three day event, I had two interventions which is when the entities work through you to heal you. This is not a physical intervention; it is a faith-healing. One of these interventions occurred spontaneously in the middle of the confusion of the first day, and the other happened consciously when I chose to attend an intervention on the last day of the event.

I did not experience the reactions to intervention that were described to us, which made me skeptical. Nevertheless, I followed the directions they gave us for what to do after the procedures. However, my hope for a physical cure upon seeing John of God never disappeared, because I believed the cure would come from another realm whether I felt it or not and whether I reacted to it in the conventional way or not.

I returned home, and although I was disappointed that my hopes and expectations for "the miracle" were not met, I had learned something. I realized again that the spiritual meaning of healing is very subjective, very personal, and very cosmic at the same time.

A few days after returning, I noticed *I was* more relaxed and *I did* have a greater sense of peace than when I left for the weekend. So, even though the physical miracle of a cure had not happened, the trip was worth it.

Victor's Birth

In the Catholic tradition, each day of the week is dedicated to several saints, with some being more well-known than others. Calendars are published with the name of the most important saint for each day.

The coming baby's grandfather emailed me from Spain to let me know that the baby was expected to be born on March 8 which is, coincidentally, Saint John of God day. He knew I was going to Canada to see John of God from Brazil, and he was struck by the coincidence of the dates. As it turns out, the baby was born in Spain on March 9, but it was still March 8 in the United States at the time of the baby's birth.

After my cousin gave birth to a baby boy, my anxiety was growing day by day about going to Spain and meeting him in person. I knew I needed to go. I wanted to go desperately, but I was afraid to stop my therapies, even temporarily, to visit my cousins. Still my desire to meet the new baby was stronger than my fear. I let the oncologist know I was going to Spain. I told him I would contact him on my return to speak with him about looking for a surgeon. The truth is, I was not thrilled with the idea of having surgery. Deep inside I was not only excited about the baby; I was relieved to have an excuse to postpone my decision about having surgery.

As soon as my cousins found out I was preparing to travel to Spain to see the baby, they asked me to be the Godmother. The Godmother! They started making the arrangements for the baby's Baptism. I was really surprised. I did not think I was qualified for such an honor. The Godmother! My first impulse was excitement. My second was to reject their request.

Since I am so much older than the parents, how could I be responsible for the baby's upbringing in the event that something would happen to them? Also, they already have a large extended family in Spain to take over the care of the baby. And, I live so far away. And, what about the fact that I am no longer exactly a Catholic? My cousin knows me very well, and she may think I am well-educated in the Catholic religion, especially since I was a nun at one time. But, is she also aware of the extent to which I have moved on from Catholicism? That spirituality is now my religion? My "religious" commitment now is to grow spiritually every day. I want to have an open mind. I want to be accepting of people of all religions and beliefs. How would the parents react to that?

Well, here is how they reacted: They called me on the phone and told me that the reason they wanted me as Godmother was because I was the symbolic representation of an open mind. I was an open window to the world and everything that this means. Although the baby would be raised in Spain, they wished for their son to be open to the world. They wanted him to become a world citizen. What's more, they considered me to be the best person in the family to bring this awareness to him. I was floored. So here I was—becoming a Godmother of a brand new baby.

"I'll do it!" I said.

The Universe was not only giving me a child but a mission to perform on his behalf.

This was Life! This was the power of the new! A world was beginning and I was going to be part of it.

I went to Spain.

Oh, how it felt to hold that newborn baby. Baby Victor. So soft and new and innocent. So pure. So beautiful. To hold him in my arms evoked brand new feelings. Oh, life… life… life.

The concept of death had infused my whole being for so long—in fact for my whole life, and now suddenly, here I was holding Life. In my very own arms, I held the bright new future.

Back from Spain

Shortly after arriving home from the airport, I fell down stairs causing some pain in my right shoulder and arm. I looked into my Recall Healing reference book, and sure enough, there was the explanation. I was back at home, stuck again in my situation and unconsciously resisting moving forward.

I still couldn't decide whether I wanted to have the surgery, but based on all the information the oncologist gave me and the fact that my lymph nodes were swollen, I was afraid the cancer had spread. I needed to know for certain before I made any decisions. I decided I would have a PET scan, and depending on the results, I would contact the oncologist afterwards to look for a surgeon. Since my doctor had denied my request for a CT scan, even though it was recommended as a follow-up procedure to the PET scan done a year earlier, I decided to go ahead and pay for the PET scan myself. I just could not face contacting my doctor and getting another denial again.

They emailed a copy of the PET scan results to my "alternative medicine doctor" and a copy to me. When I read that they could not find anything in the thorax, I could not believe it and kept looking to see whether the report had my name on it or someone else's. Well, the report did have my name on it and I decided to continue reading. I was really grateful to learn that the tumors in my abdomen that were found to be benign a few years earlier, still appeared in the scan unchanged, which was proof to me that they actually had examined the scan report and it was *mine*. Indeed, this was not a mistake. My PET scan showed positive test results.

In spite of reading the report, I did not trust my English and emailed it to a couple of my American friends. I asked them to confirm what I was reading. Maybe, after almost two years in doubt, I was still in denial. Maybe I was denying that I could be cancer-free, even that I could be happy! And useful! And wanted! And loved by my family—not to mention responsible for a brand new life.

It took a while for the news to sink in. I felt disoriented, like being in a fog. I didn't know exactly what to do or how to stop the treatment trajectory I had been on—which was no longer necessary. I didn't know how to give thanks.

I spoke with my alternative medicine doctor in the U.S. and then with my doctor in Mexico to give him the news. This doctor recommended that I should go to a third doctor, Dr. Daniel Beilin, who specializes in full-body Thermographies which, he said, would be the best method to maintain my health. Everyone involved in my care agreed it was critical to maintain my immune system and make sure it was functioning properly. It was time to move on to a maintenance program. So I started seeing this new doctor too. I have never failed to do whatever was recommended to me or whatever I felt was necessary to take care of my physical health, my emotional health, and my spiritual well-being. (Also, I do believe in miracles. I do!—which is the reason I went to see John of God).

My doctor in San Francisco knew me better than my doctor in Mexico, and he knew that because of the result of my PET scan, I was not going to suddenly start "eating sugar and steak." I never had done that in the first place, although since having cancer, I have made changes in my diet and lifestyle that will be permanent. My doctor in Mexico still wanted me to continue with some therapies, but in the end, we all agreed upon the kind of program I should follow. They slightly reduced the number of supplements I was taking. But, I must admit that after almost two years I felt so attached to the pills it was hard to take fewer. The pill-taking had become my *meaning:* my *healing process.* I had had a similar sensation after my open-heart surgery. I was afraid if I exercised, my fast heart beats might come back. Now I was worried that the cancer might appear again at any moment—if I did not continue the full course of treatment.

As soon as I fully digested the news, the first thing I did was to send an email to everyone I had notified when I was first diagnosed. At that time, I had asked them for prayers for my recovery and now I asked them for prayers of thanksgiving. We could now close this chapter of my life.

10

MY TEACHER, MY HEALER

People have asked me what healed my cancer. The same day I was diagnosed I stopped all sugar in my diet, something I will continue for the rest of my life. I also stopped the small amount of chicken I had been eating. (I do not eat red meat.) Before knowing what treatment I would choose for my cancer, I started immediately with vitamin C IVs. Then, I spent two weeks in a Mexican Clinic doing Aloe Vera, vitamin C, B17, Poly-MVA IVs, hyperthermia, sauna, coffee enemas, SPDT (sound and light treatments), a vaccine made from my urine and many other treatments. After I came home many of these treatments continued, not to mention the number of pills (supplements) I was taking and I still take every day.

However, over time I had realized, more and more, that what would really heal my cancer would be to know the cause of it. When I was diagnosed, I had the first inclination of the cause. As I delved deeper, more causes revealed themselves. Little by little I began to understand the nature of these causes. Eventually, I began to release the causes from the cells of my body.

Now I know very clearly that my healing started before I was born. Before I was born the doctors said I would not survive birth. I did survive, but, as it turns out, I was born with a "defective" heart. My heart was so sick it completely restricted my activities. My life became set apart from others. I became so isolated and depressed that I spent many years just wanting to die. In fact, Death became my life's "project purpose." As I mentioned earlier, in the theory of Recall Healing, each of us has a major life "project purpose"—and mine, from before birth until I healed from cancer, entailed living in a continual dance with Death.

All through the years though, my body managed to stay alive. I believe my body stayed alive so my heart and soul might have a chance to heal.

First my heart began to teach me how to heal, then, my cancer carried my healing process further. If it would not have been for my sick heart, I probably would not have taken the path of physical treatments I chose for cancer. Had it not been for my heart, for example, I would have chosen the common path of surgery and radiation. Because I feared having radiation so close to my heart, I was inspired to take a different healing path. Surgery and radiation therapy would have been a faster process; perhaps it would have taken three months. But now I see I needed much more than three months to heal. Healing is a deep process; it requires arriving at a deep understanding.

Recall Healing stresses that in order to achieve healing, first we must *recognize* what caused our illness, second we must *articulate* and *understand* the cause and, third, we must *release* the cause. When we release the cause of our illness, we can truly heal that illness. Releasing the cause is a process that goes far beyond simply alleviating the symptoms. That is why I say we can be "cured" without being healed—and we can heal without being cured.

I was diagnosed with cancer. I asked myself, "What has caused this disease?" I knew immediately: it was the ship. When I began to contemplate all the problems and stress the ship had caused, it led me to think about my husband and my marriage. The last years of my marriage had been turbulent. My husband had bought this historic ship thirty years earlier—and one stormy night it sank where it was moored. My husband raised it from the water. He repaired it. After several failed attempts to sell it, the ship came back to us. Little by little the ship became like the "other woman" in my marriage. She stole my husband from me a little more each day. One day I found out—in public—that we owed the half a million dollars he had borrowed to fix her. Because I had no knowledge of the expenditure, I felt completely betrayed by him. The ship situation became a total drama. It put our home nest at risk. Now we were financially insecure and, in addition, I was suffering from the psychological trauma of "losing" my husband. My brain responded by creating cancer: my brain created more cells within the lobular tissue of my breast.

Recall Healing says that it is common for a woman to develop lobular cancer of the breast when the behavior of her spouse puts the future of the nest in jeopardy. I was not an exception. We thought our problems would be solved when we sold the ship and were able to repay the debt. However, after my husband's death, the new owner reneged on the contract to buy the ship. He abandoned it and I was left to deal with a whole new set of issues alone. Then, to make matters worse, the ship was stolen from me. Finally, I had to release the ship from my life.

Further, my cancer was located in the outside of my breast. According to Recall Healing, when a tumor appears "near the outside," that means that the causes of the cancer are events that enter you from the outside world. Here is how Dr. Gilbert Renaud explained it to me:

As a right handed woman, your cancer was in the three o'clock position in your left breast. This could indicate that you have had an important stressful experience coming from a "situation outside your nest," a situation that potentially puts the survival of your nest at risk. The location of the cancer also touches the "horizontal line" of the breast. The horizontal line is at the same level as the nipple. This could indicate that you were strongly connected to your "rational mind" from the beginning of your life. Indeed, in order to survive your mother's attitude, and then later your husband's, you learned to live more in your "rational mind" than in your "subjective mind," which helped you to avoid suffering. Your "subjective mind" is your heart.

This explanation made total sense to me. In those moments when I did connect with my heart, I would inevitably burst into tears. Becoming aware of how deeply hurt I felt by the behavior of the people closest to me became an important element in my inner process to heal myself.

My healing awakening started, however, with an inanimate object: the ship. As I would come to learn, in Recall Healing theory and in dream theory, a ship or boat is symbolically associated with the mother. Recognizing this connection caused me to think about my mother which made me realize how estranged we were from each other all our lives. As a little girl, I felt like I was stranded on my own island. I never felt my mother's love or protection. We didn't understand each other. My mother, strong as she was, could not understand how her own child could be so weak. I remember her saying, "You do not seem like my daughter." That is because I was always sick.

My mother put an end to my dream of going to the university and she tried to block me from going to the convent. We drifted more and more apart.

One day, when I was studying the personality types outlined by the Enneagram, I suddenly saw my mother as a "type." She was a number Two on the Enneagram which meant she was the Giver, the Helper. That meant her strength would be Humility and her weakness would be Pride. This made sense. My mother's pride was what allowed her to survive in the world she grew up in. Suddenly, I was able to understand my mother's behavior. With knowledge comes understanding. Understanding brings appreciation. Now I could see my mother as the little girl whose father died when she was seven years old. I could see my mother as the little girl who was expected to leave school to take over her father's job as a shepherd. I could see her as the little girl whose job it became to help her bereaved mother maintain a household with five little children. Malnourished and illiterate, my mother, throughout her life, could rely only on her innate physical strength to survive. That physical strength served her well—until the day I had to put her in a nursing home. She had advanced osteoporosis. She had just had unsuccessful surgery for a broken femur and she was going to be in a wheelchair for the rest of her life. That was the day my mother and I switched roles. She became the weak child who had been left alone. I became the strong one—but now I lived half way across the world. I would not be able to be there for her. So, the separation between my mother and me was not to be resolved. In my heart, that was the day I began to say goodbye to her and, as I said goodbye, her life began to flash before me.

As my mother's life flashed before me, my life began to flash before me too.

In my mind's eye, I saw myself as the little girl rejected by her mother for being weak. *Feo, Feo, Feo.* I saw this little girl who thought of herself as different, if not ugly. I saw this little girl who was rejected by the other children because she was too odd, because she was a sick outsider, because she didn't have the capacity or the permission to play. I saw a little girl whose precious lamb was killed by her own family—and she had no idea why. I saw a little girl whose favorite uncle was snapped away from her by the jaws of death. I also saw the pre-teen being sexually abused in her own home. I saw her abuser, the artist, who damaged her relationship with art—just as the girl was beginning to love art. On the screen of my consciousness, I saw the young woman denied entry to the university and the young woman who could not qualify for the job she desired as her second choice—all because her heart was defective. For this young woman, not even second choices were possible. Yes, she was angry.

All of these are the reasons I had desired death all along. Death would be my redeemer.

First my mother's life flashed before me, then my life flashed before me, and all of a sudden, as I stood there in the nursing home on that final day before returning to the United States, my heart began to crack open. My heart cracked open, love began to trickle in, and then it began to flood. I began to love my mother and I began to love her child. The longer I stood there, the more intense the love became. That was the day a new kind of tears began. As I cried, I began to release the pain and sorrow and suffering of all the years of my life.

As I saw my mother's life clearly—and then my own—I saw all the contradictions in both of our stories. I saw the way each of us had evolved.

As a young weak woman, I had gone to the convent searching for a spiritual life. I had always felt closer to the spirit than to the body. From the very beginning, my body had betrayed me and life circumstances had betrayed me even more. Little by little I had drifted apart from living until the only thing that seemed important to me was Spirit. That was why the difficult material challenges of a cloistered Discalced Carmelite nun of that specific order—an order which had separated from the main branch of Discalced Carmelites so they could maintain the customs and habits of the time of St. Therese of Jesus—were not obstacles for me as they would have been for others. For example, putting on the twenty-two pound habit we had to wear every day all year long, winter and summer, was just routine for me. It was natural. Getting dressed was not a problem, nor were any other "inconveniences." In fact, I was completely neutral which felt more spiritual to me than material. I felt no gains and I felt no losses no matter what happened. Indeed, I was envious of whoever I saw in a coffin. Finally, they had arrived at the destination. I thought they were lucky. It seemed so hard to be alive.

I entered the convent because I wanted to escape having to live in the world. I was hoping to be able to live in Spirit. However, what I found is not what I was searching for. Rather, in the convent I found a group of nuns who were happy. They were alive in their bodies. They lived fully and laughed often. They enjoyed every minute of their existence. Well, how was *I* going to fit there? It became clear to me I was going to have to leave. A convent is no place for a dead woman walking.

I did leave the convent—eventually. One more dream had come down.

And, now, with hindsight, I can see why life took me there: learning all the virtues I learned in the convent would help me to be able to deal with my future. The discipline I learned in the convent would help me face a troubled marriage and years of cancer treatments in solitude.

Ironically, the sexual abuse that turned me away from art was what brought me back to it again—and with much more appreciation than before. I had to make such an effort to look at art in the years just after the abuse—because of the association it brought—that now I know my love and enjoyment for art is far superior than it would have ever been if the sexual abuse never would have occurred. Had the abuse not happened, I would have taken art for granted. I am really grateful now for the joy and happiness art brings into my life. Also, I now realize that though I hardly know anything about the person who abused me, he, too, probably had been abused. Now I actually can feel compassion for him. Generally, none of us has an easy path.

During all this time examining my life, I wondered why the sexual abuse caused so much damage to my relationship with art and none in my relationship with men. I came to the conclusion that I was very lucky to have the father I had and the uncle I lost when I was seven years old. They both were strong figures and role models in my life. My father showed me what it means to love. I was always safe with him. I was safe with my uncle too—and I was my uncle's beloved child companion—especially every Sunday when he took me to the park. I felt very close to them and my love and appreciation for them was able to override whatever damage the molestation might have caused. I had only been lightly exposed to the art world by my father in childhood, and now I was trying to get in touch with it on my own. Because the art world was not solid to me at that time, the damage happened there. If the Universe challenged me with my mother, it did bless me with my father.

Going even deeper, I realized that my husband, who I saw as the one who had betrayed me—the one I lost to the ship—was the same man I had fallen in love with. He was the same man who brought me to a new country; the man who offered me a new life. This was the man who also brought me self-esteem. I can see that so very clearly now. Bob was able to see an exquisite value in me and he insisted on me seeing the value in myself. Too, he gave me all the freedom in the world to discover who I was. He was always there to hold my hand when I made a mistake. He supported me in my weakest moments. Bob helped me to become who I am today. That is why I chose the song "Because you loved me" by Celine Dion to be played at his Memorial Service.

> *You saw the best there was in me*
> *Lifted me up when I couldn't reach*
> *You gave me faith 'coz you believed*
> *I'm everything I am*
> *Because you loved me.*

As I mentioned earlier, I played that song the day before Bob's Memorial too. That day I had my own private Memorial Service for him. While playing that song, I wrote pages and pages reviewing our whole life together. I wrote about how, the first time I saw him, it was love at first sight. I wrote about how we maintained our love at a distance until we married, then about how we planned and built our home. I wrote about how the ship became the shadow in our marriage. *Bob, you were the strong one at the beginning of our marriage but our roles changed as time passed by. I became stronger and you became weaker, especially as we aged and our age difference became more apparent. Our marriage disintegrated because of the ship but then we tried so hard to put it back together—especially when we had that big party on the ship to share in celebrating your dream come true just five days before you died.* As I wrote and wrote, I put closure to all of our differences. I wrote and wrote, wrote out our whole lives together and then I collected our most memorable pictures, including the pictures of Odin, Shiva, and Mittens. I put the letter and all the pictures in a big thick envelope. *Before the casket was closed I put that envelope in your inside pocket, the pocket next to your heart.*

The writing and reviewing of my life with my husband made me see the whole picture of our relationship, a picture of love and commitment, renewal, celebration and support. A new sense of love and appreciation for my husband engulfed me.

I grew up in a Catholic country and, although I was not raised in a devout Catholic family and I did not attend Catholic schools, meeting the nuns in England resulted in my going into the convent. My marriage to a non-practicing Jewish man and moving to a new country made me see the Catholic Church from a new perspective. My view of spirituality broadened. My interest in learning, which is what has kept me going all my life, started opening more and more doors for me. I studied the Enneagram and dream theory and I entered the Psychic Horizons school. My continuous work with the Enneagram in my own life and in my relationships, not to mention my dream journal and all I learned at Psychic Horizons, gave me the preliminary tools for my healing process. Later, my metaphysical studies through the *Tarot of the Spirit* and Kabbalah enhanced that process greatly.

The Catholic religion of my childhood transformed into spirituality. My new spirituality, which emerged as a result of my metaphysical studies, became the turning point in my healing. This was evident when I went to see John of God. When I saw John of God, I was still expecting a miracle in the way I had been taught to expect a miracle as a child. Yes, I went looking for a miracle to happen to me. When I went to see John of God, I already knew intellectually that I was made in the image of God. But, what happened there was that I experienced this belief on the cellular level. I came back with the unassailable knowledge, that I, myself, am the image of God. I am the healer. I, myself, am the miracle. Upon my return, I had the great revelation that my project purpose had shifted: my project purpose had been Death. Now it was Life.

One night, as I was driving home from Kabbalah class contemplating the stars and the full moon, the same clarity I was seeing in the sky suddenly invaded the feelings of my heart. My heart opened like the sky and I burst into tears. Suddenly, I had a feeling of clarity I had never felt before. I realized that, in the end, my mother had died, my husband had died, the ship was gone and the little girl with the broken heart was no longer. It was all gone. That was all in the past. Now I would begin a new life. I found myself talking to my mother. I asked her to help me on my new road: *"Mamá, ayúdame."* *(Help me.)*

In that very same moment, the moment I asked my mother for help, I had the realization that all the contradictions in my life— and the illnesses—were resolved. How could this be? I realized in that moment, on the cellular level, it is not what happens to us that initiates illness in our lives, but rather illness is caused by how we react to what happens. How we react makes us sick and, furthermore, how we react also heals us.

It was time for all my ordeals to end. I had found *Life* and now I wanted to live. Ironically, I realized that *cancer is what kept me alive* while I was searching for *Life*.

Suddenly:

> *I saw my mother and I felt compassion.*

> *I saw my husband and I felt compassion.*

> *I saw my abuser and I felt compassion.*

> *I saw myself and I felt compassion.*

I was overcome with love. I loved life. I loved life immensely. Suddenly, I loved all my relations and the whole of the world. By the time I arrived home that night, I was healed. I knew I was healed deep down inside. I arrived "home"—the place I started. I was where I began and yet I was changed. I had reached my destination—my

Source.

In writing my story I was compelled to remember deeply. Everything came to the surface. It came to the surface in revelations and tears. I cried, understood, and released, cried, understood, and released. I released the energy of over sixty years. When you can hold the whole story, I now understood, when you can hold all the contradictions and see that every single thing is perfect, you are healed. That is what it means to be healed.

I am still on a boat with my cancer. But there has been a big shift. Being in the company of the tiger has changed me. The tiger still looks into my eyes, but now we understand each other. I am no longer afraid. Life no longer scares me, nor does death. Here is what I have learned: not only am I not going to die of living—like that little girl with the hurting heart—but I will live in brilliant aliveness, even if we are all dying every day.

Now I sit on the boat, healed, but still facing the tiger. I still have a lump in my breast. I might have surgery to remove it. I do not know what the surgeon will find. I have no way of knowing what the future will bring. None of us do. But I have learned something. As I faced the tiger—my cancer, my teacher and my healer—he taught me how to come alive. He taught me how to recognize what was killing me. He taught me how to release the cause of the illness. And, finally, he taught me how to enter the dance of life.

It may seem ironic that the dance would begin with a tiger. He who might destroy me showed me the way to become whole.

EPILOGUE

A Tree, A Book and a Baby

Feeling so uncomfortable in this world and looking forward to death was the underlying theme in my life. I always felt like a leaf blowing with the wind, a leaf unattached from a tree. It is as if I had been disconnected from the Tree of Life even before I was born. As I explained in this book, death became my life project purpose. As such, I was determined not to leave anything behind when I die. Not for a moment would I have even considered writing a book, having a child, or planting a tree.

Well, here I am writing a book in the hope that my journey with cancer may inspire and help others.

Too, I have a new baby. My new baby is calling me back to the Tree of Life. My new baby is calling me home. He is calling me to reattach to the Tree. My dearest darling Victor, here is my message for you:

> "Victor, your life has just begun. The fact of your birth is the very spark that ignited the fire of life inside me, a fire which was dormant until you were born. Your mother chose to call you Victor in honor of your grandfathers and your great-grandfather, and what no one knew was that your name would also mean the "victory" in the challenge of my healing journey. You brought me happiness even as cancer, my teacher, showed me the way to become vibrantly alive."

I do not have a green thumb. I have never been successful growing plants. I could never imagine myself planting a tree. I have never been particularly connected to nature and would not know where to begin to grow something. Well, listen to this. Here is the last story I want to tell you: Sometimes I arrive early for my appointments with Pamela, my Kabbalah teacher. Often, I will take a detour through a small lot I own near her house. For years, even as I did not pay much attention to life itself, I did not pay much attention to this land. As I was passing by one day, I saw a redwood tree growing right in the middle of the lot. The redwood: ancient, majestic, the heart of the coastal rainforest. This was a strange sight because there are no redwoods or redwood groves around this area, and it is a mystery as to why this tree decided to grow in my lot. But now I understand why I always rejected the Tree of Life itself. No wonder I was not aware of the redwood growing on my land. Now the Tree of Life is calling me home—to my new self, she who celebrates life.

Fog and fire are key elements in the reproduction and growth of a redwood tree. Ironically, I had spent a good part of my life in a state of permanent fog which prevented me from living life to the fullest. But in the same way that fog holds humidity to allow the redwood to access sufficient light to grow and become the tallest tree on Earth, such humidity, over time, bathed my heart and my soul. It was under these conditions I was able to keep my interest in learning and growing spiritually all my life.

Regarding fire, redwood trees must burn to go to seed. When the mother tree has been damaged by fire, new redwood trees sprout from burls left around the base of the trunk. Cancer burned me to the ground. It was the burning that created the foundation for my new life to sprout.

Through cancer, my teacher, my healer, I found Life and the

experience of God. By planting the redwood tree, God acknowledged the process I had been through with cancer. Now the sacred redwood stands as a glorious monument to healing and spirituality.

As the Universe was the force that planted the physical redwood tree, I planted the spiritual one. Cancer brought me a life which will continue to expand long beyond the time when my journey is complete and I have arrived back to the Source.

Victor, this book is for you: I give you my book, beloved child. And may God continue to grow our mighty tree. May the bountiful Tree of Life continue to blossom forever.

ABOUT THE AUTHOR

PHOTO BY TAMARA TREJO

Manuela Sherman was born in Madrid, Spain in 1949. She was born with a heart defect which impacted her health throughout her life thus she was no stranger to illness. But when she was diagnosed with cancer at age 61 in 2011, she began to discover a process of healing that was previously unimaginable. Not only did she learn how to heal herself, she learned the secret to the true nature of the healing process which she shares in this book. *CANCER, My Teacher, My Healer* is her first book. She can be reached at www.manuelasherman.com.

PHOTO BY HIROMI MOTOJIMA

A TREE, A BOOK AND A BABY

ACKNOWLEDGMENTS

First and foremost I want to thank Pamela Eakins. She is the one that saw this book in me far before I was aware of it and she is the one who had the knowledge, intelligence, patience and love to bring it out of me. I will ever be indebted to her for the long hours she spent with me helping me put it all together. She encouraged me and had faith in me. Without her this book would have never happened.

To Clara Ellen, who from beyond, saw this whole project and pulled strings for it to happen.

To Janet Moulin for her patience in correcting my English, especially for the long hours we spent on the phone discussing grammar and meanings.

Many doctors helped me during the course of my healing. In particular I want to thank Dr. Gilbert Renaud and Dr. Daniel Beilin, who I talk about in this volume.

I would like to thank the many friends old and new. To my old friends, I appreciate your support along the way. Thank you to the new friends I met along this journey. Some had cancer, some didn't. Some are still with us, some have passed away. Without their inspiration I would have not written this book.

Last but not least, thank you to my family in Spain, especially to the new baby, Victor, who is changing my life.

73349582R00081

Made in the USA
Columbia, SC
10 July 2017